Swagger at 60

Use the Tools of Mental Toughness to Serve and Succeed at Any Age

Lee Witt

*Always,
Keep goin' strong!*

*Lee Witt
2019*

Published by BookLocker.com, Inc., Bradenton, Florida.

Printed in the United States of America on acid-free paper.

BookLocker.com, Inc.
2014

First Edition

DISCLAIMER

This book details the author's personal experiences with and opinions about personal growth and aging. The author is not licensed as a psychologist or physician.

The author and publisher are providing this book and its contents on an "as is" basis and make no representations or warranties of any kind with respect to this book or its contents. The author and publisher disclaim all such representations and warranties, including for example warranties of merchantability and business advice for a particular purpose. In addition, the author and publisher do not represent or warrant that the information accessible via this book is accurate, complete or current.

The statements made about products and services have not been evaluated by the U.S. government. Please consult with your own legal or accounting professional regarding the suggestions and recommendations made in this book.

Except as specifically stated in this book, neither the author or publisher, nor any authors, contributors, or other representatives will be liable for damages arising out of or in connection with the use of this book. This is a comprehensive limitation of liability that applies to all damages of any kind, including (without limitation) compensatory; direct, indirect or consequential damages; loss of data, income or profit; loss of or damage to property and claims of third parties.

You understand that this book is not intended as a substitute for consultation with a licensed medical, legal or accounting professional. Before you begin any change your lifestyle in any way, you will consult a licensed professional to ensure that you are doing what's best for your situation.

This book provides content related to personal growth and business topics. As such, use of this book implies your acceptance of this disclaimer.

Leadership exists when one sacrifices his own self-interests for the benefit of those in his charge.

This book is dedicated to those who sacrifice and serve so that others may have a future – and to my son Landeau, for whom the future belongs.

CONTENTS

INTRODUCTION

A few years ago, best-selling author, media personality and former Navy SEAL, Richard Machowicz, was doing a radio interview. The host asked Mack, "What's in the future for you?" After giving a few details of his many projects, Mack said, "I want to make the last thing I ever do, the greatest thing I ever do."

Isn't that terrific? How many of us have the stones to say such a thing?

Now that I'm 60 years old, I'm taking Mack's statement to heart. I'm taking it as a personal challenge. But taking this ultimate challenge requires a certain mental toughness. And this toughness must be continually developed. I can't slack off or slow down. If anything, as we age, we need to work towards even greater strength. As such, I've written this book as a manual for myself moving forward. Now that it's published, I have to hold myself accountable or be branded a hypocrite. My hope is that all of us can live with the idea that the last thing we ever do can be our greatest. And no matter how old we are, we can use the tools outlined in this book to be successful.

Most of us are familiar with the high-level principles of being successful. But sometimes the day-to-day grind beats the greatness out of us. It happens to all of us. And it's in those times that we need to dig into our mental toolkit and come up with a strategy. This book will give us the toolkit to do just that.

At its base, this book is about service. In order to stay significant and relevant, we must be able to, as Bob Dylan said a half century ago, "Serve somebody." The mental toughness tools in this book will give us the means to carry on in service when it's uncomfortable and we just don't feel like it. We often believe that we need to be inspired. Inspiration helps but in reality, we simply need to be disciplined. *We need to be able to get up and do the things we don't feel like doing when they most need to be done.* That's what mental toughness enables us to do.

Service is also an incredibly important concept because it implies that we don't live in a vacuum. Service prioritizes the well-being of other people, which is not always easy. And sometimes, prioritizing others doesn't make sense. But if you have the stones to attempt making the last thing you do your greatest, there's an even chance that you will be providing a service to someone.

In addition to service, this book is also about being superior. It's not about having a superiority complex. I'm talking about *actually becoming superior.* Yes, this implies comparison with others. If that is distasteful to you, I would ask you to consider this. It is superior people, products and services that have made our life what it is today. Advancements in medicine, travel, business and communication are only available to us because superior human beings invented superior products and made them accessible.

Mental toughness enables us to work towards both service and superiority at any age. It enables us to build strong, daily habits that propel us forward. It's those habits that kick in when we're not inspired and motivated. Because let's face it, we're not always motivated to get up early. We're not always motivated to go to the gym. And we're not always inspired to do what we know is in everyone's best interests.

So what's the actual definition of mental toughness? Many books will tell us that mental toughness is made up of grit, perseverance and a never-quit spirit. They tell us that we need to exercise such concepts as control, commitment, challenge and confidence. But often that's as far as they go. There are rarely any tools as to how to put those qualities into action. They just say, "This is what you need. So go out there and be confident and tough!"

For some people, that's enough. But I've found it useful to describe specific behaviors that can help you "act out" those qualities and "be confident and tough" in practice. What does it actually look like to be confident and tough? And how do I do it?

For our purposes, we'll define mental toughness very simply. Mental toughness is the ability and willingness to call forth the necessary energy, skills and capacities we need in order to accomplish our goals, particularly when things are difficult. And it's those very skills and capacities that we'll address in this book.

People who are mentally tough keep their minds in the game when others panic or check out. I've watched people in difficult business situations throw their hands up and say, "It's too much, it's too overwhelming! I can't deal with this right now." Then they storm out of the room. They prefer to run away and avoid the issues.

In fact, *right now is the best time to deal with the issues because it's the only time we have*. Right now is where life is lived. Mentally tough people stop and take control of their minds the very moment they hear themselves use the word "overwhelmed." They do not panic. Nor do they explode in a useless angry tirade that serves no purpose. Tough people handle and take charge of their minds in the midst of pressure. They catch themselves when they're about to panic and they slow down their thought process. They might even ask themselves, "Am I okay right now? The answer is almost always yes. Then they ask, "What is the one thing I could immediately do to improve this situation?"

If no solution is readily apparent, the answer might be to just simply breathe. Deep breathing is a mental toughness tool that slows us down. It puts us into a better state, and that's a place where better decisions can be made. It provides an opportunity to step back and consider the situation. We often discount breathing because it's so natural. Yet try doing anything without it.

It's the tools of mental toughness that allow the most successful people to catch themselves and make productive choices in real time. Once we begin to approach what I call "mental toughness mastery," we begin to choose personal fulfillment in circumstances where others fall apart. This is a difficult place to get to, but it is a place that's available to all of us. It's a constant struggle for me. But I remind myself that I get to choose how to manage my own mind. No one can take control of my mind without my consent.

The 7ᵗʰ Inning Stretch

At 60, most of us are in the last third of our life. I call it the 7ᵗʰ inning of a nine-inning game. Even if we've reached the bottom of the 7ᵗʰ, we still want to feel significant. And there is still more game to play! The tools of mental toughness can keep us relevant to the very end, no matter how young or old we are. But yes, there are times when all of us feel small, weak, and insignificant.

I remember my father at sixty-three, just a few years older than I am now. He had spent his life as a teacher and a coach. While coaching football and basketball, his life had been characterized by robust physical challenge and active sports. Now he was lying in a hospital bed, having undergone a quintuple bypass operation on his heart. For good reason, he was feeling weak and helpless.

The doctors were not overly optimistic about his recovery. It was maybe fifty-fifty.

Shortly after his surgery, I noticed that around his bed were flowers and little stuffed animals brought by well-meaning friends and family. While very thoughtful, these gifts did not create an environment conducive to what an adult male of the World War II generation would have considered masculine. In my early thirties at the time, I decided to try something.

As opposed to tiptoeing into his room like everyone else, I strutted in with some swagger. With a voice louder than it needed to be, I said, "My God, Dad, you sure are a tough old son-of-a-bitch! But you didn't have to go this far to prove it!"

His demeanor changed almost instantly. All of a sudden, he had an identity to live up to. He was still a man in someone's eyes who could demonstrate toughness. He could use his circumstance to see himself as a tough guy, hanging in against the odds. Even from his hospital bed, he could show others how to deal with difficult circumstances. I could feel his energy shift.

I tossed a couple of stuffed animals into the corner and said, "Jesus, let's get this crap out of here and put the game on."

It was a chilly October evening in 1986. I turned on the World Series above his hospital bed. Together, we watched the Mets battle the Red Sox. The Mets rallied. So did my dad.

He lived another nine years after doctors were talking in terms of days. I'm not saying that my strategy was the reason he carried on. But feeling significant and that you still have something to teach or do can sometimes keep the motor running past its expiration date.

It's our ability to be of service and add value that keeps that motor running. That's our challenge as we age. Armed with the tools outlined in this book, we can all stay relevant and strive to make the last things we do the greatest. That's my plan, anyway. I hope you'll join me.

SECTION I:

SWAGGER AND SERVICE

CHAPTER ONE – *Serve with Humility but Act with Swagger!*

"What would you do if you were besieged in a place entirely destitute of provisions?' asked the examiner, when Napoleon was a cadet.

Without hesitation Napoleon replied, "If there were anything to eat in the enemy's camp, I should not be concerned."

What? We're supposed to have swagger at 60?

No. *We're supposed to be humble at 60.* We're supposed to have taken so much punishment that the sheer absence of pain equals pleasure. We're supposed to be grateful that we still have the energy to watch television. We're supposed to shuffle through life with our humble heads bowed hoping that no one runs into us and knocks us over.

Well, screw that. We already know plenty about humility. Humility comes with age as part of the natural process. If you're keeping score, humility is undefeated. It's built in. And if we're lucky to live long enough, we'll get to put that diaper back on. We'll all be humbled in due time.

Don't get me wrong. Humility has its place. I'm all about *serving* with humility. There is no job beneath me. We do whatever needs doing. There is dignity in every kind of human labor.

But here's where I draw the line. I'm not a fan of humility as an attitude or a lifestyle. By the time we're 60 years old, we know all about humility. And while we've won a few battles, we've also been beaten many times in business, relationships, and sports. We've taken just about every kind of punishment you can think of. Individually and collectively, we've been excoriated in public and on social media. And we've no doubt been somebody's punch line more than once along the way.

We've worked twelve hour days that turned into 84 hour weeks. We've gone through bankruptcies, divorces, heart attacks, angioplasties, bypass operations, mammograms, prostate exams and more colonoscopies than you can count. We've battled to put ourselves and our kids through college. Now our grandkids are looking at us like we're ATM machines. And if we're fortunate enough to have parents who are still living, they probably need our assistance as well. For many of us, retirement isn't even an option.

So I say, "Serve with humility, but act with swagger." Yes, I'm looking for people with swagger – or who want to get some. With so many people still counting on us, and our paycheck, why wouldn't we have a little swagger? *We have earned it*!

I'm looking for people who are giving the middle finger to the limitations that come with age and finding ways to beat those limitations. That's what this book is all about; *making our capabilities triumph over our limitations so that we can continue to serve and contribute.* And if we want to stay relevant, we need to contribute.

This isn't a new concept. But it's one worth revisiting. Why? *Because we've normalized limitations.* We've normalized comfort. And in the process of normalizing these things, we've also normalized obesity, depression, addiction and attention deficit. Whatever you've got, we've normalized it. In the process, we've gotten fat. We've gotten impatient. We've gotten rude, lazy, whiny and too weak to handle the smallest inconvenience. Heck, it's too much trouble for most people to flip on their turn signal while driving!

In short, we've gone soft.

Now I completely understand if you don't like my attitude. I'm sure I sound preachy, smug and perhaps even intolerant. I get that. But in fact, I'm none of those things. (Well, maybe a little smug.) But that doesn't and shouldn't diminish the quality of the message. If we continue to argue on behalf of our limitations, we will continually justify our weakness. The normalization of limitations has broken our willpower, which a certain part of academia seems to believe doesn't even exist anymore. (Yes, I've read all of the studies around glucose and willpower. I understand the data and we'll get to that.)

So what's the answer to all of the above-mentioned afflictions?

Swagger. Yes, swagger. Now I'm not suggesting that you be obnoxious – although if you can back up your swagger with results – good for you. I'm simply suggesting that if you've experienced any or all of the adversities I mentioned above; if you've gotten through the bankruptcies and the illnesses et cetera, and you're still breathing, you deserve to strut a little bit. You get big points for just hanging in there.

In the Introduction, I mentioned former Navy SEAL, Richard Machowicz, who is actually a very humble, but dangerous guy. He believes that the difference between success and failure comes down to your ability to focus on a target. Mack says that things like fear, self-doubt, hesitation, second-guessing, fatigue, and pain are typically what get in the way of our ability to focus. As such, those things keep us from succeeding. I contend that putting a little swagger into your step can help you overcome the kinds of doubt and second-guessing that he's talking about. We'll get into the physiology and energy of just how that works and the science behind it in later chapters. It's by no means the entire answer, but it's a start.

The very fact that you have a pulse means you're still in the game. And if you are still in the game, you can get things done! You can get healthier. You can still make things happen. And if you're 60 years old and you're awesome? Don't apologize for it. Never dumb down or apologize for being outstanding. Don't shrink to make other people feel better. Seriously, stop it! Inspire them and challenge them to want to elevate their game so that they can play at your level.

Last year, at age 59, I overheard a woman a few folks behind me talking in a grocery line. She was talking about me. She whispered to her friend, "What's with that guy? Wearing a tank top and showing off his muscles like that. I don't understand people like that."

Well, for one thing, it was ninety degrees outside. But that wasn't the point. I got out of line and pleasantly walked back to her which, of course, shocked her. With a big smile I said, "Hi, my name is Lee. I'm 59 years old." (She looked appropriately surprised to hear my age, which was gratifying.) "I wanted to address your comment in order to perhaps share a different perspective."

I continued. "Here's the deal. You want me to apologize. You want me to apologize for wearing a tank top and being in great physical condition. Yes, I have muscles. I deliberately worked my ass off to get them. And I'm never going to apologize for having had the discipline to be in the gym four days a week for 42 years running. I'm also not going to apologize for having the discipline to have spent another 25 years avoiding the kinds of pseudo-foods that are in *your* shopping cart. In other words, I'm not going to apologize for looking really good and being as fit and healthy as my gene pool allows. Is there some unseemly vanity in that? Probably. But I'm human and every now and then, I like to bring the Ferrari, that is, my body, out of the garage. So, having shared this perspective, I hope that you have a wonderful day."

As I walked away, I couldn't resist turning around and saying, "Oh yeah, I'm also available for personal training whenever you're ready."

Then, being a gentleman, I walked to the back of the line that I had voluntary left.

I share this because I want all of you to have a story like that one. Essentially, that gal made my day. The rewards of discipline and willpower far outweigh the rewards of the cheesecake she would no doubt be eating later. (There's that smugness again.) But nothing tastes as good as a great body and terrific health feels. And while I'm writing this primarily to document my own progress and to catalog the tools of mental toughness, I'd love to have anyone, of any age, join me in the quest for greater awesomeness.

It's never too late – and it's never too soon to begin.

It's all about right now.

Okay, where'd I leave my swag...

CHAPTER TWO - *I'm Bringing ~~Sexy~~ Sixty Back!*

"Hard pressed on my right. My center is yielding. Impossible to maneuver. Situation excellent. I am attacking." –

- Ferdinand Foch at the Battle of the Marne

I believe that if *we're not dead, we're not done*. This book is about leveraging our years of experience to make whatever is left of our lives count. Like Ferdinand Foch in the quote above, we can always consider ways to attack, no matter what the challenge before us.

You need never apologize for getting older. And if you've worked hard and want to kick back into retirement for a well deserved rest, I have no quarrel with that. But if your pilot light is still burning and you believe that there is more to do, this book will help you overcome some of the limitations we face at *any* age. You don't have to be a member of the AARP to benefit from this book. But I've written it with that demographic in mind.

Not too long ago, I recall performing Justin Timberlake's terrific song, *Sexy Back* with my band,

BrickHouse, in a Seattle-area casino. As I was singing, it occurred to me that within a couple of years I could change the words to *Sixty Back!* At one time, being 60 years old and performing in an R&B, Rock, and Top 40 band would have seemed ridiculous. Some of you may still believe that. If so, I'm going to challenge you to change your mind. Along with several like-minded seniors, *we're bringing sixty back!* (If you're having a difficult time visualizing this, think Springsteen, Petty or Sting. As of this writing, they're doing quite well.)

We already know the benefits of proper exercise, nutrition and rest. There are countless books, trainers and gyms available that can help you learn what you need to know. I encourage you to explore those. An excellent book to consult is Richard Sullivan's <u>Reclaim Your Youth: Growing Younger after 40</u>.

Health is my greatest value and exercise lays the foundation for everything that I do. Without good health, it's hard to make the most of your life. That's a given. As such, we won't beat that theme to death. Most of us know what we need to do.

But if we know what we need to do, *why aren't we doing it?* Whether it's nutrition, fitness, business, or relationships, we typically know what we need to do in order to be successful. The information is out there. Yet too often, we just don't act upon what we know. That's a function of what is happening from the neck up. That's what we'll deal with from here on out.

What we will address are all of the mental toughness tools that can help us make our capabilities overcome our limitations. And regardless of what some self-help gurus might say, we all have limitations. But no matter what age we are, we can improve. We can get better. That's part of what makes being human interesting. Research shows us that there are a number of tools that can help us overcome fear, inertia and self-sabotaging behaviors. These tools can make us mentally tough at any age. To my knowledge, no one has documented all of them in one place. Over the last twenty years, I've made a comprehensive study of these tools. This book will outline what I've found. I've drawn heavily from the highest achievers in business, sports, music, science, and the military world of special operations. I owe all of these contributors a debt of gratitude. Several of these folks and their books are listed in the Appendix.

The idea of reaching the upper limits of my genetic potential has always appealed to me. And it's always directional. We never reach 100% of our best in any area – but we can still work hard to approach it. The closer we come, the more fun!

It's worth remembering that we can add value to our environment at any age. In any job or community, we will never be the victim of age, race, or religious discrimination if we are adding so much value that they can't live without us. Excellence and being of service always wins the day.

The Perception of Age

It would be useful to change the perception of what it means to get older. Our culture champions youth and largely dismisses anyone over the age of fifty, let alone 60. I contend that our society ignores the following statistics at their peril.

According to the July, 2014 edition of AARP Magazine, there are now 100 million people over the age of 50 in the United States. This age group will soon have more than 70 percent of the disposable income. They buy two-thirds of all new cars, a third of all movie tickets and half of all computers sold. They spend about $7 billion each year shopping online. More than 80 percent of all premium travel expenses are traced to their credit cards.

As a result, the over-50 population in the U.S. ranks as the third largest economy in the world. Only the entireties of the United States and China have a greater gross national product!

Yet, when my phone rings and someone conducting marketing research asks for my age, he hangs up when he finds out that I'm 60. Despite these stupefying statistics, marketers don't want my money. According to Nielsen, only five percent of advertising is aimed at older consumers. For example, people 75 and up buy five times as many new cars as people 18 to 24. Yet, how many older people do you see in a car commercial?

These statistics indicate that we're not done simply because we can order off the back page of the Denny's menu. But we must continually show up and earn what we get. We're not entitled to privilege simply because we're older. We need to contribute and make a difference.

I should also say that I absolutely love our nation's young people. I love them because of the culture of tolerance they're creating. They have helped us eliminate so much of the prejudice and discrimination that was prevalent when I was growing up. In so many ways, they are much more enlightened than my generation. So it's important to point out that I'm a big advocate of our nation's youth. But I'm also an advocate for those who want to contribute at any age.

Fortunately, I'm around people of all ages while working my day job in the aerospace business. We have a nice mix of generations in our office. As you might imagine, there is a lot of fun banter. Recently, when talking about my cover band, BrickHouse, one of my younger colleagues began teasing me. He said, "Hey, you're definitely a rock star in your own mind."

I responded, "Well of course I am. That's where it all begins!"

It all begins in the mind. And we'll begin there as well.

It's All Made Up!

Think back to when you were two days old. You don't remember, do you? Of course you don't. You don't remember because you had no language. Language is what enables us to label and understand concepts. In essence, your mind was a blank slate, waiting to absorb whatever it was taught.

Why is this important? It's important because *we have learned* almost everything that we believe. Our parents, our teachers, pastors, priests, coaches, counselors and friends, in conjunction with books, TV and movies, have influenced who we are and what we believe. And it is language that has allowed us to integrate these teachings and experiences.

I have learned through the study of psychology, philosophy, business, military instruction, athletics and the most advanced self-protection training on earth – that we put ourselves at a tremendous disadvantage when we simply "buy in" to the social and cultural conditioning that we've been exposed to since birth.

We have been molded with positive and negative reinforcement, propaganda, and marketing messages from day one to this very moment. And because people have a need to feel certain and secure, we believe much of what we are told. It's quite possible that many of us have lost complete touch with our own basic instincts. And this limits us severely.

We play with one arm tied behind our back when we buy into what the culture tells us to believe in and what the rules are. We have been programmed from birth to believe that things should be a certain way. But in fact, it's all made up! Isn't it?

I advocate challenging the cultural mores, assumptions, rules, patterns, and narratives that are constantly thrust upon us. People just like you have decided what the rules are. Am I telling you not to obey the rules? Not necessarily. Many rules make good sense. I'm glad they exist. I'm simply telling you to consider thinking for yourself. Decide for yourself what is ethical. Decide for yourself what makes sense. Decide for yourself what is in everyone's rational best interests. Then act accordingly.

By all means, break the rules when the rules make no sense. Many rules and social conventions are designed to limit you and keep you in line. Bureaucracies exist to perpetuate themselves, not to serve you. Be your own person who makes his own decisions.

How many times have we heard someone say, "I did all of the right things. I followed all the rules. I did what everyone said I should do!" And they're broke, tired and miserable. Take heed. Many of history's greatest inventors and achievers broke the rules and we are the beneficiaries.

We have been programmed and conditioned since birth. In order to gain favor with parents and teachers, we needed to behave ourselves and get good grades. Now, as adults, we are labeled as selfish social deviants if we don't follow all of society's conventions, expectations and social mores.

We were not taught to think for ourselves. It's just that simple. But we can start now. It's never too late to begin forging our own path. Sometimes it's worth considering that "if you make the rules, you don't have to break the rules."

For those of you thinking that I'm suggesting anarchy; that's ridiculous. Nor am I implying that we justify egregious acts of violence. But it's worth pointing out that even the ancient Aramaic scripture in the Bible (also written by humans and subject to the limitations of language interpretations) doesn't say, "Thou shalt not kill." It says, "Thou shalt not do murder." There's a difference. If it comes down to me or the other guy, I choose me. I call that justifiable homicide.

I've actually had conversations with folks who believe that the law is sacrosanct and should never be violated. These authoritarian personalities have forgotten that laws are made by people. When challenged, the law is interpreted by The Supreme Court – also a group of…wait for it…that's right – people! And it's worth remembering that The Supreme Court gave us such landmark verdicts as the Dred Scott decision, which basically told us that slavery was cool. Well, *it's not!*

I'll take my own conscience, thank you.

Having said this, keep in mind that behaviors have consequences and breaking rules may come with some. Accept that – and remember that it's in no one's best interests to do harm. But *you* are just as capable of deciding what is or isn't harmful – or ethical. Think for yourself.

Still not quite with me? Here's another example. If you are from Northern Ireland, whether you are Catholic or Protestant depends solely upon which side of the street you are born. You do not *choose* to be Catholic or Protestant. It is chosen for you. Like people in that environment, it's quite possible that our entire belief system has come as a result of the conditioning and programming handed to us by family, religion and the popular culture. It was explained to us, through language, who was good and who was bad. We were told what was right and what was wrong. And it made sense to buy in because the people telling us were providing us with food, clothing and shelter.

This is good news because if our beliefs aren't serving us, we can change them. If we are miserable, we're probably adhering to rules that go against our very human nature. But in the same way that we can delete our Internet history, we can wipe our own slate clean. We can hit the reset button and begin at zero. Even at 60 years of age, we can start from a blank slate and create a belief system that can turn us in the direction of anyone we want to be, provided we're willing to put in the effort. Providing we have the tools to be mentally tough.

Certainly, humans have instincts and biologically-driven genetic predispositions toward survival that are not learned. They are innate. But when it comes to thinking and cognition, the human race began as a blank slate. Language has allowed us to communicate on a sophisticated level. We wouldn't understand our own religion, political affiliations, values and beliefs if we didn't have language to make sense of them. In other words, they wouldn't exist. So rather than simply accepting the programming and conditioning that my mind may have adopted indiscriminately, I have the ability to take charge of the programming that runs in my own mind. After all, *it's MY mind!* And if that's not the case, I'll send whoever *is* in charge of my mind off to therapy – and I'll get better!

Some of the Cultural Conditioning/Programming We Face

We don't have to buy in to the pervasive cultural programming (read brainwashing) that tells us that:

- I have to be loved and can't possibly be happy if I'm alone.
- I have to play the social network game and be "validated." (Validation is for parking.)
- I have to be responsible for the happiness of the people around me.
- I have to join "the consumer culture" and have the latest and greatest of everything.
- I have to be afraid.

This programming is designed to sell us things, make us feel guilty and to buy into other people's agendas. These other agendas need not become our agenda, unless of course, that's what we willingly choose. But we should never let other people convince us that we're not okay. (It's simply more programming.) All of the blathering about "what we need" is designed to put money in the pockets of people whose agenda is to tell us that we will be happy when we buy what they're selling. They are telling us that success, happiness, and satisfaction exist "out there" – somewhere outside of ourselves.

Our consumer culture has programmed us to believe that the quick dopamine fix of a new pair of shoes or the latest smart phone is the way to happiness. No, it's the way to instant gratification. Now, instant gratification has its place, particularly if you have a lot of disposable cash. I love instant gratification. But let's not confuse instant gratification with happiness. It's called "instant" because it's going away shortly. Then, in the next instant, you'll need something else. The cycle has the potential to perpetuate itself until your credit card debt is insurmountable.

Happiness is another matter. It typically involves living a life of meaning and purpose that provides a contentment that permeates our days. That's something that marketing professionals find more challenging to sell.

Apart from various marketeering efforts, people (and therapists) will also try and tell us that we're sick, weak, and codependent. They will tell us that our innate drives for food, sex, wealth, power and other natural human tendencies are not normal, or at least, not healthy. In my mind, they are neither bad nor good, they just are. It occasionally might be in our best interests to control them and balance them, but these innate drives give us the impetus to create value and become successful.

To fight societal programming means to go against an entire cultural drift. It specifically means, among other things, soothing our own bad feelings without the help of others, pursuing the goals that we choose, and standing on our own two feet. It often means going it alone. Because we are largely social beings, this can be challenging. For most, it's just easier to go along with the herd.

The people and advertising agencies promoting their agendas love the "herd mentality." They would tell us that we are only "good" and "worthy" people if we do what they tell us to do. Any move towards independent thinking is scoffed at, ridiculed and crushed.

Buying into this brainwashing leads to risk aversion, collectivism and an exaggerated emphasis on political correctness. We can only combat this Orwellian cultural programming by mastering ourselves and our sensory impulses with the tools of mental toughness that we'll outline in Chapter Four. It requires listening to our own instincts and standing apart from the herd. In doing so, we must also be tolerant and allow others the same courtesy to make their own choices. If we expect tolerance from others, we must grant it as well.

The bottom line is simply that we can choose our own mental programming. (After all, it's all made up!) We can choose mental toughness and not allow others to control how we think. We can write our own script. Life is an artist's canvas and we are the artists. Certainly, we can respect the choices of others. But we still reserve sovereign power to design ourselves. No matter what age we are, I suggest that we live by design, not by default. We can choose to change our identity and reinvent ourselves at any time. We still have the power of choice. What goes on in our own heads is our own affair.

CHAPTER THREE – *Don't Be a Cynic: Be a Better Room Badass!*

"I strive to be consistent, dominant, and clutch."

- Russell Wilson

A while back, I was watching ESPN. Football analyst and former NFL quarterback, Trent Dilfer, was talking about current Seattle Seahawk quarterback and Super Bowl champ, Russell Wilson. Russell is a much beloved figure in Seattle (my home) and Trent was, in part, explaining why. He explained that when Russell Wilson comes into a room, the room gets better. His positive spirit and can-do energy permeates every room he enters.

I believe that kind of spirit and energy is available to all of us at any age. But we have to have the intention to bring it. It's really about showing up in the moment with awareness and the desire to be of service. I call it being a "Better Room Badass." I first witnessed this spirit many years ago when I met a young woman named Cassandra.

The Cassandra Story

I love "the Cassandra Story" because it's true and it applies to everyone in every walk of life. This story reminds us of just how much power each of us really has. And by power, I'm really talking about influence and our ability to serve others. I'm talking about the power to turn misery into magic, not just for other people but for ourselves as well.

Let me tell you the story.

It was the mid 1990's and the fact that I can recall it so well is an indicator of the immense impact it had on me. It was back when I had a little more hair. That's important to the story because at the time, my wife was trying to talk me into going to a "hair stylist." A "salon" if you will. Now I've always been kind of an old school guy, more of a barber shop person – you know – the kind of shop with the candy cane pole out in front. (They probably no longer exist.) But I thought, hey, if this is what my wife wants me to try, it's not such a big deal, a small sacrifice really. So I looked through the yellow pages (this was before the Internet) and I found a place called Heavenly Hair Stylists. Seriously, Heavenly Hair Stylists. It made me laugh so I called them up and made an appointment for 1:00 o'clock on a Saturday.

Truthfully, I was kind of dreading it. This just wasn't my thing. But on the day of the appointment, I put my coat on and headed out. It was December and it was pouring outside, a miserable day. The wind was gusting up to 40 miles an hour and I was getting wetter by the moment. I was running some Christmas-related errands, mailing packages at the UPS store and picking up various odds and ends. As it happened, I arrived a little early for my appointment. I had a bit of a sinus headache and I just wanted this haircut business to be over. To add insult to injury, when I parked the car on the side of the street, I had one of those TV commercial moments when, honest-to-God, a truck drove past and splashed water from a puddle up all over my pants. So now I'm soaked from the waist down, I've got a headache and I'm going into a place where I figure I'm not going to feel comfortable. But I walked into Heavenly Hair Stylists and was immediately greeted by a nicely dressed young woman, probably early to mid-20's.

"Hi," she said. "My name is Cassandra. Oh you poor thing, you're soaked. Let me take your coat."

She hustled me over to a waiting area and plopped me into a recliner lounge chair. There was a television on. She must have read the kind of guy I am because she immediately put the channel on a college basketball game. I noticed on the table beside the chair was just about every kind of magazine imaginable, a USA Today and the local newspaper.

Now this is where it started to get interesting. Cassandra said, "Would you like a glass of red or white wine?"

"What?" I couldn't believe I was hearing this. I started looking around for the hidden camera. She repeated the question and I said, "My God, it's one in the afternoon."

She said, "Would you prefer a soda?"

I said, "You wouldn't happen to have a beer, would you? The kind of day I'm having, a nice cold one might just take the edge off."

Within a few minutes, she was back with a cold beer but that was just the half of it. As God is my witness, she also had a hair dryer that she plugged in and began to dry my pants as I reclined in the chair."

I said, "Cassandra, do you do this for everyone?"

What she said next really stayed with me. She said, "Lee, I want to make sure that for everyone that comes in here, this is the BEST part of their day – and the part that they'll remember." That struck me as an interesting concept.

She then said, "I've made that my job because I love making people happy and making them feel special."

"Well so far it's working," I said. I was thinking of proposing marriage but that job was already filled. Now what I didn't realize at the time was that she had actually gone out a back door, run across the street in the pouring rain and bought me a beer at a store with what I assume was her own money because she only had wine and soda in the shop. But I didn't learn this until much later.

So I got my haircut. The stylist was male and he was pleasant enough, but when he was done, he called out for Cassandra.

About ten seconds later I heard this buzzing sound that sounded like an electric razor. But it was one of those massage contraptions and Cassandra was running it across my back, neck and shoulders. I was in complete heaven and I thought well maybe that's where the name Heavenly Hair Styling comes from. I mean, by the time I left, I was just a happy drunk blob.

I said, "Are you guys open on Sundays? I'd like to come back and get another haircut tomorrow."

I was fascinated by what was happening here and I asked her about all of this.

She said," I love feeling so powerful. I have the ultimate power to make everyone's day. It's not a job for me, it's a calling. When you came in here, you were wet, cold and miserable. Now you're relaxed, happy and cheerful – and maybe a little buzzed."

Cassandra was exercising *real* power. She had begun as a receptionist and just expanded her own idea of customer service and taken it to a new level. In essence, she had created her own position in customer relations. Cassandra turned my day around and in doing so, in her own small way; she turned my life around as well. She completely changed the way that I looked at power. But that wasn't the end of it. She took my business card (I'd have given her my wallet had she asked) and a week later, I actually got a thank you card from her in the mail.

My wife was very pleased that I was no longer reluctant about going to the "salon." She was however, a little concerned about how frequently I wanted to go back.

For us, the most important point of this story is not just that Cassandra was great for business – which of course she was - but that she was having the time of her life watching the expression on my face with each new way she could find to surprise and delight me. By herself, she created an entire environment. Instead of just taking phone calls and making appointments, she worked to create fun for herself and everyone.

Some years ago I asked the owner of the shop whatever happened to her. She told me that she now owns a chain of styling shops in the Midwest.

Cassandra didn't have a college education but she knew more about business than 95 percent of the MBAs I've ever met. She understood that the business of business is people. I forget that sometimes and I have to remind myself. We think it's just about collecting money. But in any business, we're participating in a people sport every day. And that's hard sometimes. It requires a certain intentionality and resolve to remember that we have the ability to create an environment. But the beauty of this is that the ability to create an environment doesn't require an MBA or a Ph.D. *This is something that's available to each of us, no matter our age!* Cassandra got that. And she turned it into a really nice living for herself.

She recognized that she had the *power* to turn misery into magic.

So after I'd gone back to Heavenly Hair Stylists about three times, I made it a point to continually ask Cassandra what she was thinking about when she went about creating this extraordinary environment. She really boiled it down to three main points.

She said:

1. We can influence people by the way that we show up. That's where the power comes from. Showing up! I think that's even truer today. We have so much technology yet in many ways, we've lost our humanity. Cassandra made it her personal mission to be the one person people remembered that day. Cassandra taught me that no matter what you do, if you play it world class and show leadership in everything you do, you will succeed on a massive level. She didn't need a title to be a leader. She just called herself the CEO of herself. In essence, we're all that. We are all the CEO of ourselves. We can show innovation and leadership from wherever we're at and at any age. For Cassandra, the styling shop was her theater and everyday was *show time!* Maybe there's a way that we can make our work our theater and our business a stage. Each of us has the opportunity to provide a service – or we can provide an "experience."

For me, it's every handshake, every conversation, every client phone call, every seven second interaction with someone who asks me to sign a book, every speaking opportunity, and every employee interaction. These are all potential moments for show time! Maybe this is a little over the top. But can we not agree that it's better to err on the side of showing up big time and providing a positive experience for the people we're interacting with as well as ourselves?

2. We can leave people better than we found them. When I showed up at Heavenly Hair Styling, I was a mess. I was soaked, cold, had a headache and was in a bad mood. When I left, I was none of those things. Cassandra completely turned me around. She was an "artist" at making people feel good. In fact, she was the Michelangelo of making people feel good. People want to do business with people they like and trust and who make them feel special. Cassandra taught me that kindness is free. Listening to customers and answering their questions costs nothing. Not doing those things can be very costly.

3. We can decide to be the most fun, effective and solution-oriented person in every room that we're in.

Now I said, "Cassandra, this seems like it might take a lot of energy." She said no. Just decide. That's all it takes. And why not? She said, "I'm going to be here anyway. It doesn't take any more energy to have fun than it does to be miserable."

She was right. Studies show that we are co-creating each other's biology all the time. Emotions are contagious. We can infect others with our attitude. We can become an infectious disease! Imagine the environment you could create right here if you took on this attitude.

This is what Trent Dilfer was talking about with Russell Wilson. His attitude is infectious. His energy is bigger than other people's and it changes lives. He is definitely a "better room badass."

After all, who are we not to be brilliant, fantastic, fun and amazing? If we know that emotions are contagious, we can influence people by the way that we show up.

We can leave people better than we found them. And we can decide to be the most constructive and can-do people in any room or area that we're in. That's power. That's influence. And we can't help but succeed and contribute if we do those things consistently. As we grow older, practicing these three main points can give us a competitive advantage in any area of life.

Beware Cynicism or "The Curmudgeon Factor"

One of the difficulties of being a senior member of society is that we've seen and experienced so much. I catch myself being cynical when, over a quarter of a century, I watch the organization in which I work decentralize, centralize, decentralize, and centralize over and over again. Each time, the proponents act like it's the first time it's ever happened and they've come up with a great new idea.

It's in these times that I try and become very self-aware. I attempt to catch myself whenever I become "the cynical curmudgeon." Why? Because cynicism doesn't work. It makes no difference whether my opinion is right or wrong. Nothing great has ever been achieved through cynicism. Cynics are typically critics. Critics typically produce nothing. Following this logic, we can say that cynics produce nothing. I don't want to be that person. Plus, the non-cynics are generally the ones who are mentally tough enough to push through fatigue and failure.

Certainly, it's fine to point out where experience tells you that an idea might not work. I will express myself, but then try and figure out a way to help. If I can't do that, I at least step back and stay out of the way. As Hippocrates said, "First, do no harm."

At 60 years of age, we have seen and heard a lot. But it's important that we don't impede progress, or even the perception of progress. Change happens, even if it's recycled.

Beware Bitterness, Self-Pity and Victimhood

Like cynicism, bitterness is also a useless waste of psychic energy. It is a concept mostly characterized by self-pity. Self-pity accomplishes nothing and there is no room for it in our philosophy. Mentally tough individuals will never accept being the victims of circumstance. The mentally tough find ways to prevail over their circumstances, making their capabilities exceed their limitations at every turn.

Retired four-star General Stan McChrystal, who turned sixty in 2014 recently said, "I think people are a little bit like nations. Every once in a while you're going to take one in the head, and you're either going to feel sorry for yourself and go sit in the corner of the dugout and cry, or you're going to get up and fix your problems."

Having spent three days with General McChrystal and his CrossLead consulting team, I can tell you that they're all about fixing problems and finding solutions. There is no place for self-pity in their mindset. And if we are going to be leaders or set any kind of example, we must not waste a second on it.

SECTION II –

THE TOOLS, MASTERY, AND THE CODE

CHAPTER FOUR – *The Tools of Mental Toughness*

"At no point in life does being younger help you. It comes down to this. I'm either tougher than you, or you're tougher than me. And we're going to find out."

Chael Sonnen – Retired Mixed Martial Arts Fighter

It's now time to get into specific mental toughness tools that we can implement to help us get the results that we're after. These tools will help people of any age succeed in any undertaking if practiced with diligence.

In a culture that is evolving with an increasing reliance on new technology, these tools are particularly useful. Why? Because for the time being, *our extraordinary capacity to invent new technology has exceeded our human capacity to manage it.*

While that may seem like a bold statement, the evidence is compelling.

The majority of humans are fat. I'm sorry, they just are. Technology has made physical movement and exercise practically unnecessary. Most of our lives no longer require physical labor so exercise must be deliberately scheduled. In addition, technology has allowed us to package and deliver processed foods in abundance. Food is everywhere – and not everyone can afford the technology offered by liposuction.

The majority of humans cannot focus. Technology produces constant distractions. As such, humans are continually bombarded with another tempting shiny object to pursue.

The majority of humans do not recognize how much potentially productive time they waste in technology such as social media, television and simply idle gossip.

The majority of humans no longer read books and many struggle with literacy. As such, they have limited frames of reference, limited vocabularies, and do not know what they don't know. Technology has obviated the demand for literature.

The majority of humans cannot comfortably sit alone in a room with nothing to keep them occupied for even 15 minutes. Being left alone with their own thoughts without distraction or entertainment creates an incredible sense of unease and even panic.

It's quite possible that technology will deliver answers to the above concerns at some point. Until then, the tools of mental toughness give us the human capacity to manage ourselves and take back our own lives.

The most important tool that we can initially pick up is the "offensive mindset."

Tool 1: The Offensive Mindset

"It's always less risky to do it than to have it done to you."

- *U.S. Navy SEALS*

There are two kinds of people. One kind wakes up in the morning and asks, "What's going to happen to me?" The second kind of person wakes up and asks, "What am I going to get done?"

Do you see the difference? The first kind of person is taking a defensive and reactive posture. You can almost feel the fear inherent in the question. The second kind of person is aggressively *attacking the day*. This is a much more productive approach. If you adopt an offensive mindset, you are acting upon life before it can act upon you. This proactive stance puts you in a far more powerful and constructive position. Plus, it's bold and not fear-based.

Most fear is essentially a form of exaggerated self-talk that comes from answering that first question, "What's going to happen to me?" Internally, we're answering that question based upon things that we think we know. As the conversation unfolds, we begin to think about and dwell upon all of the things that could possibly go wrong. Of course, in reality, *we don't know* what's going to happen.

But it is our mind's job to help us survive so it's typically going to run worst-case scenarios. Much of the time, what we worry about never occurs. So how do we get past this fear-based conversation? The aforementioned Richard Machowicz teaches that *the way out of fear is through focus.* According to Mack, focus occurs when concentration, clarity and action converge in the present moment to create a result. In short, focus is the doing of the thing that must be done right now.

This leads us back to our offensive mindset question that resonates through Mack's teaching. *"What am I going to get done?"* When we are concentrating on executing the task that needs doing, we are too busy being engaged in the process to even remember that we were afraid just a moment ago.

Most people take a wait-and-see attitude when problems first crop up. But that's a defensive posture. Waiting might be the best strategy once we've weighed alternatives, but it should never be our default position. We should always be examining the situation to seek clarity and look for solutions. Then we work to get out in front of the problem and take appropriate action. Our default position should always embrace the idea of moving forward. Be a cause, not an effect of someone else's move. Attack!

To the best of my knowledge, a man named Jerry Peterson first coined the phrase, "offensive mindset." Jerry came up with this concept as part of a system of self-protection and martial arts embraced by such notable organizations as the U.S. Navy SEALs. The idea of an offensive mindset fits very nicely into our paradigm of "it's all made up."

Peterson postulated that our language, which we control, creates the basis for this mindset. Consider these two columns of words:

React	Act
Defend	Attack
Block	Strike
Evade	Penetrate
Follow	Lead
Try	Do
Fear	Courage
Wait	Go

Unlike the words in the left column, the words in the right column are proactive, aggressive words designed to propel us forward. And forward is where progress lives. There is absolutely no reactivity in those words. Choosing the words on the right when thinking and speaking will more often make us the cause of something – and not an effect of something being caused.

It's worth noting that the words we use hold three major possibilities. First, some words, like those in the left column above, come with a sub-code of fear. Thinking and speaking these words lead us into uncertainty and hesitation. The second kind of word is neutral. There is no emotion involved. Third are the words that have a sub-code of fearlessness. These are the words in the right column.

Words have an emotional content and we are in control of the words we think and say. Later in this chapter we will learn how the tools of visualization and meditation can help us become aware of the words we use and how they can propel us towards massive achievement. Once we become aware, we have the ability to choose among options.

Up to now, it's quite possible that many of us have spent our entire lives in a defensive, reactive position. If so, it's because practically everything we absorb from the moment we wake up is promoting fear and doom. The morning news is replete with worrisome information. Even the traffic and weather reports are based on "the dangers to watch out for."

Each morning, I receive MSNBC news headlines on my computer at work. These are just some of the headlines

I received on July 1, 2014. This is just one brief dose of fear conditioning from one random morning. We are inundated with these headlines daily.

Forget the Fireworks? First Hurricane of Season Could Ruin Fourth

Hiker Doesn't Buy a New Phone That Saved His Life

Unprecedented: French Ex-President Held by Cops

Businessman Arrested Over Schoolgirls' Abduction

'Staggering' Numbers Dying in Iraq, UN Says

Teen Beaten to Death Over Video Game: Pal Indicted

Breaking Point: Teens' Murders Trigger Grief and Fury

ISIS Threat to US Targets 'High' Say Officials

As if this is not enough, have you ever watched CNN's "The Situation Room" with host Wolf Blitzer? In any five-minute segment, you will hear words like tragedy, devastation, emergency, crisis, panic, jobless, homeless, car bomb, danger, scandal, tsunami, hurricane and threat. Only the strongest, most self-aware, mentally tough people can come away from watching this without thinking Armageddon is just an hour away.

This is why we have to take control of our minds. Our minds are like empty cups but they have evolved to pay attention to threat and danger in order to ensure our survival. When we fill our minds with these "Wolfisms," we can't help but be affected, particularly if we're not aware that we're being brainwashed. Committing to an offensive mindset helps us to consciously recognize and counter this programming. And I'm not debating the accuracy of what Wolf is saying. I'm simply suggesting that the mental model it promotes does nothing to help us move forward aggressively towards our own targets. It trains us to be tentative, hesitant, and scared. And it's solely designed to get viewers to pay attention and buy what CNN's advertisers are selling.

The media is not the only cultural phenomenon teaching fear. It permeates every facet of society. We are taught defensive driving because the other guy is no doubt crazy and we need to be afraid. We are taught to communicate to others in such a way as to not offend them. We are afraid they won't like us. And of course, we are taught to defend ourselves if verbally or physically attacked because we are afraid of being hurt or killed.

As you can see, much of our life is based upon fear and defense. I'm not suggesting that all of the above examples are inappropriate in their intent. But it's worth considering that there might be another way to look at all of this.

Let's go back to the words in the right and left columns above. If we find ourselves using the words in the left column more than those in the right, why is that? If we feel defensive, reactive, afraid, and like a follower more often than we feel like a proactive, courageous leader, why is that?

I suggest that it begins with our mindset and we can change that beginning today.

Abraham Lincoln was perhaps the first proponent of the offensive mindset. He suggested that the best way to predict the future is to create it. That's the essence of the offensive mindset. It's almost always best to make the other guy adjust to you, rather than you adjusting to him. You set the agenda and execute on it. If your agenda is service-oriented and has everyone's best interests at heart, you harm no one and everyone wins.

Simply stated, it's better to be the hammer than the nail. Continuous relentless offense is the best defense. In fact, well executed offense will most likely make defense unnecessary. If we are always waiting for something to happen, it's possible that we'll be waiting a long time. And really, how much longer do we have?

Remember, waiting is not a decision. Waiting is waiting. We too often fall victim to the ready, aim, aim, aim disease. Former hockey great Wayne Gretzky was right when he said that we miss 100 percent of the shots we don't take. So take the shot!

Proofread the email once and hit send.

Make the phone call.

Pull the trigger!

Go!

Applying the Offensive Mindset to a Job Search

There is ample evidence that employers prefer to see "offensively-oriented" language on résumés and applications. Action verbs and achievement-oriented nouns are typically the most useful. According to careerbuilder.com, these are the terms hiring professionals love to see in order of preference:

Achieved
Improved
Trained/mentored
Managed
Created
Resolved
Volunteered
Influenced
Increased/decreased
Ideas
Negotiated
Launched
Revenue/profits
Under budget

These are not passive words. All but three of these items are action verbs. They are proactive words that demonstrate successful action. They indicate how we have aggressively pursued our targets. The root of the word aggression is "to move toward." It's often been associated with violence but that's just one application of the word. You can aggressively and actively pursue the things you love and positively contribute to whatever environment you're in.

If you are over 60 and looking for work, you should have a lifetime of successes to promote. Use everything and again, do not apologize for being awesome!

When the Truth Hurts

Remember our concept of "it's all made up?" One of the things we are told by the rule makers, *who've made it all up*, is that we should always tell the truth. Generally, that's a good idea. But not always. In fact, very few of us get through an entire day telling nothing but the cold-blooded truth.

If you are a smart, capable, competent, industrious senior member of society and you're not getting hired, it might be time to put the truth to bed. Most employers, understandably, want to invest in younger people who they believe are going to pay off over the long term. But the fact is, everyone has become mercenary these days and if you still believe in the "30 years and a gold watch concept" – you are sadly behind the times.

Most kids hired out of college today have one thing on their mind, going to the highest bidder. They are looking for the employer who can provide the best overall financial package. And who can blame them? They've been raised watching the insanity of Wall Street and the gluttonous avarice of corporate executives who vote themselves compensation that is inordinately disproportionate to the returns they provide stockholders.

As such, people in their twenties have no compunction about jumping from one company to the next. And they are right for feeling that way. A company is not a person. A company is usually a for-profit entity. It doesn't care. It has no feelings and it is not going to look after you. That's your job. It's best to begin that right now, no matter how old you are.

Somewhat ironically, employers who think that their investment in youth will pay off over time are getting burned. Companies invest in youth, train them, and then watch them go off to work somewhere else. In reality, companies have an even money chance of getting more years out of a senior citizen. So I suggest that if we absolutely believe in ourselves and know we're going to help a company, let's *do whatever we need to do to get in the door!* Why? Because everyone wins! The company gets a great hire and we get the work we need. This is the essence of an offensive mindset.

I am not telling you to commit fraud. But if someone asks how old you are and you think it's going to be necessary to shave a couple years off in order for everyone to get a win, have at it. And yes, many companies will have sophisticated methods of verifying your age if they decide to. But the greater point here is that if you're going to do a fantastic job for them, it's in their best interests to hire you. Having said that, *I'm putting it on you to show up and be awesome.* You better be damn good at what you're telling them you can do. Or you better tell them you're terrific – and learn very fast.

If you lie about your age and you turn out to be a horrible employee, don't mention my name. That wasn't our deal. But if you use the tools of mental toughness we're outlining, you'll have a much better chance at success.

How Can I Implement an Offensive Mindset When I've Been Conditioned in Fear?

In reality, if we've spent 60 years in reactivity and fear, implementing the offensive mindset can be a challenge. And that leads to a question I'm often asked, "How can I implement the offensive mindset when I have unwittingly been trained to be afraid? How do I retrain myself?"

That's a fair question. The first thing we can do is to establish our own agenda and plan. A plan gives us direction. To be offensive, we need to have direction and to know where we are going. Otherwise, there is nothing to attack. When that's the case, we typically get caught up in someone else's plan and agenda. That's fine if we agree to it and support it. But too often, people just get swept along in someone else's plan and end up being washed around like waves in the ocean. That's a reactive stance and not optimal unless the person running the plan has our best interests at heart. And it's best not to assume that. This leads us to the second tool.

Tool 2: The Agenda, Target and Plan

"If you don't have your own plan, you'll end up in someone else's."

- Lee Witt

An offensive mindset without an agenda, target and plan is like having the greatest turbo-charged engine just sitting around or worse, taking us places we don't want to go.

An agenda, target and plan constitute the fundamentals of mastery. These fundamentals are only necessary if we want to ensure success. If we are willing to let random events control us, or luck to reign supreme, just stop reading now. You will not need an agenda, target and plan. You can buy your lottery tickets down at the local convenience store. Good luck, I hope it works out for you.

For those of us who prefer to live by design and not by default, please read on.

When talking about our "agenda," we're simply referring to what we want to have happen in our life. We are successful when our agenda is established. That's our metric of success.

Doesn't it seem a fundamental foundation of mastery that we would want to know what we want out of a day, a week, a month, or a life? The specific things that we want are called our targets. Surprisingly, many people don't even consider what they actually want, let alone commit it to writing. They believe that the carefree, spontaneous life is the way to go. If that works for them, fine. And in reality, I appreciate and value these people because I can generally influence them to help me implement my agenda and execute my plan. They often make terrific employees because like many people, they want to be led.

People are naturally hierarchical and always looking for guidance, protection and direction. This is why "pecking orders" exist. If we show up with a solid agenda, target and plan, we will often find ourselves with a group of ready followers.

Just remember: *We can't get what we want if we don't know what we want*. We can't hit a target that we can't define.

Having a plan also helps us deal with that defensive question, "What's going to happen to me?" A plan allows us to incorporate the offensive mindset. For example, having a plan might mean that we prepare and rehearse a speech or presentation that we're afraid to give until it becomes second nature. Or it might mean that we gather as much information as possible about the person that's going to interview us for a job. Or it might even mean that we gather as much background as possible about a person we want to date. That way, we'll be armed with the knowledge of what we have in common.

Creating a plan is the surest way that we can hit clearly defined targets. There are only three reasons for not creating a plan: 1) We are ignorant of how to create one; 2) We are lazy; or 3) We simply don't want to be held accountable for executing a plan.

Number three is usually the culprit. We don't want to be accountable. Here are some examples of what accountability might look like for some of us:

- Hitting our weight loss or weight gain target (I will be 155 pounds by August 1st).
- Hitting our financial target (I will make $200,000 this year).

- Hitting our targets for being on time (I will be there at 9:00 a.m. per my commitment).
- Delivering a project on time and on budget (I will deliver this software to my customer by April 1st for the agreed-upon amount).
- Showing up – Whether it's a good day or a bad day, I will show up for my job and the significant people in my life.

Yes, there is always a possibility of failure when holding ourselves accountable. But it's that very possibility of failure and loss that makes hitting our targets meaningful. Not everyone wins a trophy. That's what makes it special when we succeed and win. And if we don't win, we get up and try again. Why? Because that's what an offensive mindset would dictate. And in reality, what else is there to do?

Our plan should simply outline how we will go about hitting our target. It should say *what* we're going to do, *how* we're going to do it, and *when* we're going to do it. Also very important is *when we will be finished*. Having time parameters around our target is critical.

For example: *"I will call this client at 10:00 a.m. and be off the phone by 10:30."* Or, *"I will begin writing this book in October and finish in May."* Without including time boundaries, our plan is simply a list that will never be finished. An open-ended list will always be just that, which means, never done.

Again, we must hold ourselves accountable and that requires some thinking when creating our plan. Additionally, it's good to include some time buffers because just about everything takes longer than we imagine.

For any number of reasons, we won't hit every single target that we shoot for. This can make us uncomfortable and sometimes deeply disappointed. But sometimes, just a simple adjustment to our plan can make the difference between success and failure on the next run. And there must always be a next run because we're mentally tough and it's not over until we say it is!

Planning and Risk

Getting anything of value accomplished comes with some inherent risk. Our job in planning is to minimize that risk. In order to do that, we want to:

1. Become expert on the basic fundamentals of whatever it is we are doing. Whether it's firing a weapon, skydiving, or learning to cook, we want to remove the possibility of failure to the fullest extent.

2. Take care of the "knowns." What possible hazards, pitfalls and potential dangers can be eliminated in advance? Eliminate them. This is also called "controlling the variables." In a

competition, the person who controls the variables inevitably wins.

3. Gather other experts to form a knowledge pool. Consult them and use their expertise. How did they succeed? When it makes sense to do so, simply follow the steps that made them successful. Add your own unique know-how in the process.

4. Practice, practice, practice. And when you can't practice in reality, practice in your mind by using the tool of visualization that you'll be reading about later in this chapter.

Planning and minimizing risk was critical when I took up skydiving years ago. As such, I practiced the fundamentals of landing, steering and in case of emergency, cutting away from my main chute before pulling my reserve. Practicing these helped cut my risk of an accident. I also minimized risk by wearing an automatic activation device on my reserve chute. This device would ensure that my reserve opened if it recognized that I was falling at a certain speed. In addition, I always packed my own chute and when possible, had an expert watching me do it. Then I double-checked it.

Of course, when falling, I always pulled my ripcord before I got dangerously low. (That seems like a no-brainer, but...)

These actions gave me confidence because I knew I had minimized the risk of a catastrophic failure. I wanted to ensure that I wasn't one of the accident cases written up on the back page of Parachutist Magazine. The unfortunate tagline on too many of those was, "Cause of Death: Impact."

To the extent possible, we want to leave nothing to chance. This includes planning how things will end. We don't want someone else running off with all of the credit and the fruits of our labor – unless that's part of the plan.

In summary: Create your plan. Minimize the risk. Execute the plan.

Keeping It Simple

Jazz musician Charles Mingus once said, "*Making the simple complicated is commonplace; making the complicated simple, awesomely simple, that's creativity.*"

Simplicity is the precursor to action. And our power lies in our ability to take action. People who are mentally tough take effective action under pressure. While having options is good, being overwhelmed by them is not. Under stress and pressure, a simple plan is easier to execute than a more complicated one. Under duress, having to recall a complicated task will paralyze some people.

As Mingus suggested, there is brilliance in simplicity. Simple is good. Simple is elegant. But in an age of increasing complexity and numerous choices, how do we simplify?

Ultimately, we simplify by making our choices binary. Just like computer code that runs on 0 and 1, we break down our choices into do or don't, will or won't, are or are not. This is not to say that we should not be diligent in thoroughly understanding our chosen target. Nor should we oversimplify the details. Not at all. But once we know what we're doing, we should simplify our choices to the barest elements.

It can't get any more straightforward than this. If there are only two moves on the board, it's simple. Pick one and get rid of everything that is keeping you from hitting that target. If you want to accomplish something significant, *spend no time on things that are not all about hitting your target.*

People who scale mountains like Mount Everest spend months planning what is needed. Once they figure out what it will take to succeed, they discard everything that is not required for the journey. They get rid of every extra ounce of unnecessary load. They shed the weight. Anything that is not absolutely essential only makes hitting the target more difficult.

Like the people climbing Mount Everest, simplifying requires that we prioritize our energy and targets. It requires letting go of some pursuits in order to achieve more abundance in other areas.

All of life is a transaction. We have to ask ourselves, "What are we willing to let go of or do without in order to get what we want?" In a culture that offers us so many abundant choices, this is a question many of us are unwilling to ask. But unless we ask it, we will continue among the ranks of the mediocre, wondering why we can't finish anything of substance. Success typically means saying no to 100 things and yes to just one.

Tool 3: Instructional Self-Talk

"Just keep going."

- Bob Schoultz

For the past forty years there has been much written about self-talk. And for good cause. What we tell ourselves *is* very important. Our internal dialog can drive us forward or hold us back. In essence, it can make or break us. But I have a slightly different take on how we might more effectively approach the running dialog in our head.

We hear a lot about the value of affirmations and confident, positive self-talk. But after years of studying psychology and mental health, I'm not completely convinced that positive self-talk works for everyone. *However, I am utterly convinced that negative self-talk will keep us down forever.*

Telling myself that "I can't do something" will almost always keep me from taking effective action. Realistically, it's difficult to convince myself to act when I'm certain of failure. If I tell myself that I can't do something or that "it won't work out" – I've essentially lost the game before I've played it.

Telling myself that I'm no good also becomes a self-fulfilling prophecy. I will find reasons to back up that statement and it becomes true in reality as well as in my own head.

However, simply telling myself that "I *am* good or that "I *can*" do something is certainly no guarantee of success. We're not all built to be "the little engine that could." But I do know that I *must* take some action if I'm even going to have the chance to succeed. So what do I do when in reality, *I don't know if I'll succeed or not?*

The answer is found in something that's better than affirmations and confident self-talk. I call it "instructional self-talk."

If I'm running a great distance, I won't convince myself that I feel great by saying to myself, "I feel great." Why? Because I don't feel great and I have a hard time believing my own lies. A better statement is, *"Just keep going."* That statement pushes me forward and I don't have to lie to myself that I feel great when I obviously don't. The phrase, "Just keep going" is simple and instructional. It tells me what to do. It brings me into the present moment and takes me out of how awful I'm going to feel in the future if I keep this up. I don't have to like the instruction and I don't have to feel good doing it. I just need to put one foot in front of the other and keep going. I am capable of that in this present moment. Whether I will be capable in future moments doesn't matter. For now, I will just keep going.

Elite military units call this "embracing the suck." It absolutely sucks when you're tired and you hurt all over. It sucks when you don't believe you can go another step. But if you step into the discomfort and embrace it, it's amazing what you can get done. By acknowledging your discomfort, you can then deal with it. You will feel pain. Pain is inevitable, suffering is not. Suffering occurs when your mind runs away with your pain, telling you how awful and unfair it is – and how you won't be able to live with it in the future. This is where mental toughness must kick in and you must take control of your mind. "Just keep going" becomes the mantra. That will take you much farther than, "Oh my God, I can't stand this."

It can also help to understand that in some almost twisted way, we can begin to enjoy the discomfort. We can recognize that it makes us "special." Whatever kind of discomfort we're feeling distinguishes us from those who aren't working longer, working out harder, or denying ourselves certain foods. While others are at happy hour, we're at the gym. While others are at the movies, we're getting our book written. We can join them when we're done – but not until then.

We do these things because we crave the high of accomplishing goals and hitting our targets. We love the thought of being mentally tougher than our peers. We love to win, particularly when it's challenging. This is what it means to be superior. Again, it's not about having a superiority or inferiority complex. It's about actually achieving superior results.

"Embracing the suck" has now become a regular part of our culture's vernacular. Even current U.S. House of Representatives minority leader, Nancy Pelosi, recently used the term to encourage House members to pass a budget deal. Embracing the suck involves accepting reality for what it is. Mentally tough people accept reality, step up to it, step into it, and work through the problems of real day-to-day living.

Instructional self-talk works in every area of life. I can be sitting here thinking about dinner and how hungry I am. So I'll give myself an instruction, "Just write the next sentence."

Or I might be preparing to perform a dead lift in the weight room, I'll tell myself, "Bend your knees, keep your head up and butt down. Now, pick the barbell up and drag it against your body for maximum leverage. Go!"

At least for me, this instruction is more effective than, "I can lift this! I know I can! I'm strong and powerful!"

Don't get me wrong, those statements are better than nothing and if they work for you, that's great. But I've found that giving myself an instruction and visualizing myself doing it perfectly is far more effective than a pep talk. In addition, giving myself instructions implies that I've asked a great question, *"What do I need to do in order to be successful in this task?"* Only by understanding what I need to do can I give myself the proper instructions. It sounds simple, but not everyone does it.

If I'm managing a difficult project and I'm tired and perplexed, I will use any number of questions in an effort to break through my fatigue and confusion. Here's a sampling of some of those questions:

1) *Yes, I'm tired. What could I do right now that would rejuvenate me?* [Answers might include; a) take a walk, b) stop and breathe deeply or c) have some coffee.]
2) *Am I okay right now?*

3) *What is the one thing I could do right now that might make this situation better?*
4) *Who else has succeeded at this and might be able to help me better understand this situation?*
5) *What other times in the past have I faced a similar difficult situation and come out a winner?*

The best way to uncover productive instructional self-talk is to ask great questions. Great answers generally follow great questions.

Sometimes my instructional self-talk is as simple as 1) Stand up straight, 2) Speak clearly and 3) Breathe and bring your best energy to this moment.

Sometimes we'll put things off because we convince ourselves that we'll feel more like doing it later. But let me ask, *"Since when do we have to feel like doing something in order to get it done?"* Don't wait. We're not going to feel like doing it later either. At these times, we need to employ what psychologists call "activation energy" to get up and get moving. Give yourself the instruction that you simply need to get this job accomplished. *Force yourself to act –* particularly when you don't feel like it! I guarantee you that if your life depended on it, you could take the action necessary that you're avoiding now.

Ultimately, it always gets back to the original questions proposed with the offensive mindset, "What am I going to get done? What do I need to do?" This approach is akin to focusing on process, not outcome. And while you always want to have your eye on the target (outcome), focusing on what you need to do in the moment will guarantee greater success. This leads us to our next tool.

Tool 4: Visualization

> *"What you see is what you get!"*
>
> *- Flip Wilson*

While he wasn't actually talking about visualization, the late comedian Flip Wilson was right. What you see *is* what you get. The data on visualization is compelling. Combined with instructional self-talk, visualization can help you become tough as nails. Visualization works, in part, because it forces you to identify exactly who you want to be and what you want to have happen. It is really just mental rehearsal. Some call it daydreaming with a purpose.

But visualization takes effort. Done properly, it requires you to work. Quite frankly, I believe a lot of folks give lip service to visualization but don't actually practice it for the very fact that it's not always comfortable to direct your mind in this manner. For those who make the effort, and then back up their visualizations with perfect practice, the results are extraordinary.

My first exposure to visualization was many years ago when I read <u>Psychocybernetics</u>, by Maxwell Maltz. Maltz, a plastic surgeon, was one of the first to suggest that the human nervous system could not distinguish between a real and an imagined event. For example, people with phobias can simply imagine what they fear and begin to sweat. But we can use that same imagination to our benefit by picturing what we want – instead of what we fear.

Of course, first we have to identify what we want. (*There's that pesky agenda, target and plan again.*) Once we have our target, we can begin to visualize success at hitting it.

When my band, BrickHouse, was scheduled to play at Seattle's Key Arena in front of 10,000 people in July of 2011, I went into the arena for sound check the night before. From the stage, I looked out at all the empty seats and played through the entire show in my mind. It truly helped to have experienced that imagined "success" before the real performance the next day. I had never played such a large stage and quite honestly, it was a bit nerve-wracking. In my visualization, I saw myself performing what my instructional self-talk was telling me to do. That was to simply execute on the targets I had in front of me, one song at a time.

Those who are really skilled in visualization bring all of their senses to bear. Olympic athletes put a tremendous amount of time into visualizing success. In essence, they are laying down a mental blueprint for winning.

Experts suggest that embracing all of the sights, sounds, smells, tactile impressions and powerful emotions that accompany a successful performance will give you the best result. I have found that I actually have some difficulty activating all of these senses. I don't get very much into the feels and smells. I typically "see" and "hear" what I expect to have happen. And that seems to be enough for me.

For those of you over 60, you will remember Hall of Fame baseball player Hank Aaron. Hank was one of the first athletes to ever acknowledge the use of visualization. Hank holds the record for the most home runs hit over a career without the use of performance-enhancing drugs. Interestingly, Hank's application of the tool focused less on the mechanics of hitting and more on the strategy. Rather than think about his stance, or how he distributed his weight, or even the smoothness of his swing, he concentrated on other things. The night before a game, he would visualize the next day's pitcher and how he would pitch to him. He began by asking great questions.

Hank would wonder, "What's Seaver going to throw? What's his best pitch? How will he try to get me out?"

Then he would visualize the two of them in a variety of situations. "How will he pitch to me with men on base with less than two outs? Will he throw junk with first base open?"

Hank would then visualize himself successfully getting hits in each scenario and how he would do it. This is an excellent example of how one person implemented each of our first four tools: 1) The Offensive Mindset; 2) An Agenda, Target, and Plan; 3) Instructional Self-Talk and of course, 4) Visualization.

The other thing that Hank would do was use rituals. He would go through a practiced routine the same way before a game or an at-bat. This way, he trained his mind and body to get into a groove. He constantly visualized success, and then he actualized it.

If we think back over our lives to the most important things at which we've succeeded, whether landing a job or a relationship, it was no doubt preceded by some sort of visualization. It may not have even been deliberate. But typically, we first see in our minds what we want to have happen. We have an intention to make it so. Then we act on that intention.

The Science Behind Visualization

Within the last few years, Canadian psychologist and neuroscience researcher, Dr. Henry "Hap" Davis, has performed extensive clinical research around visualization. Using magnetic resonance imaging (MRI) equipment, we can now monitor neural activity while we imagine a scenario. This technology indicates that when we visualize lifting our left hand, the actual part of the brain that is activated when you lift it is stimulated.

This kind of MRI gear wasn't available when Dr. Maltz wrote <u>Psychocybernetics.</u> He could only speculate that the body and human nervous system could not distinguish between a real and imagined event.

In 2008, Dr. Davis hooked elite athletes to an MRI machine to watch videos of personal success or failure. Athletes watching a triumphant performance showed greater activity in their right pre-motor cortex. This is the area of the brain that plans actions. Several researchers have concluded that activating this part of the brain with visualization provides a competitive advantage that cannot be overlooked.

More recently, in 2013, researchers at the University of Oslo attempted to find out whether visualization can trigger automatic neural responses such as pupil dilation in human eyes. During visualization of imagined light, the subjects' pupils constricted 87 percent as much as they did when exposed to real light. During imagined darkness, their pupils dilated to 56 percent of their size during real perception. This study indicates that our mental pictures activate and strengthen the very neural circuits that we actually use when it's time to deliver. Even subconscious processes that control automatic responses such as pupil dilation react to our visualization efforts. Like Dr. Davis' tests, this helps us to understand why visualization is so powerful when it comes to implementing a successful performance.

We are now proving what could only previously be acknowledged through anecdotal evidence. As far back as1983, Dr. Deborah Feltz and Dr. Daniel Landers were performing extensive research on mental rehearsal studies and concluded that using mental imagery to improve real-world functioning was incredibly powerful. But we can go back even further.

In 1976, I was the subject of an experiment performed by an Illinois State University professor and psychologist. He taught me what he called, self-hypnosis. This was really just visualization in a highly relaxed state. Our target was to improve my competitive powerlifting totals. The sport of powerlifting measures how much weight you can squat, bench press and dead lift. The person with the highest total in his or her weight class wins. By teaching me to see my successful performances in advance, I did in fact improve my totals and became a firm believer in the power of visualization. But it required daily practice, something that many people simply find boring or repetitive. But if we wish to be superior, we will find the time to put the iPhone down, turn off the technology, and get into our own mind, where a vast untapped richness of potential awaits.

Since I first performed that experiment in 1976, many other studies have also found hypnotic visualization helpful. One such study involved a nationally ranked Stanford gymnastics team. The gymnasts were taught to perform visualizations under hypnosis. At the completion of the study, they were better able to execute a number of complex moves that had proved difficult for over a year. They were able to eliminate mistakes in timing, improve their flexibility and possibly, even better focus their strength.

The old cliché, a picture is worth a thousand words proves true in these circumstances. Telling your brain what to do in a thousand words can result in a very bored mind. Showing it a picture has been proven through research in brain chemistry to much more effectively hold the brain's attention.

How to Visualize

Researchers now suggest that if we can see ourselves performing the action in the first person, through our own eyes, we will be even more effective than if watching ourselves as if we are spectators. If we can see it, hear it, feel it and enjoy it, we'll set ourselves up for success in a big way. Of course, we must be able to identify exactly what constitutes a proper performance.

The more exact we are in how we want to operate, the closer we'll come to actualizing that outcome.

If I am visualizing giving a presentation, I ask myself, "How may I best serve these people and what do they need from me?" My answers to that inform my preparation, method, content and delivery.

As I begin to visualize, I see the room and the audience in front of me. I see them listening, smiling and enjoying what I have to say. I rehearse what I'm saying from beginning to end. I can feel myself confidently "holding the room" and if I falter, I give myself instructional self-talk to get back on track. I imagine some of the questions that might be asked. I imagine giving them informed, helpful answers, totally designed to give them what they need. By the time I give the actual presentation, I am completely comfortable and actually looking forward to it.

Visualizing an Identity

No disrespect to actors intended, but I've never believed that the profession of acting would be difficult. I've been doing it every day of my life. I believe that with a baseline level of competence, we can act our way into just about any role we choose. The trick is to pick the role that we want to star in.

Too many of us believe that greatness is reserved for other people. If we can suspend that belief for a moment, perhaps we can think of ourselves as great.

If I was to visualize myself as great in my mind, how would I act? How would I breathe? How would I walk? How would I speak and what would I say?

What kinds of clothes would I wear? What kind of car would I drive? Who would my friends be?

Once we have answers to those questions, we can take it all on. We can become it. What's stopping us?

The only possible thing stopping us is that we feel we're unworthy of success. We feel like imposters. Well, enough of that. We are all capable of greatness. Initially, we may feel that we're faking it but ultimately, we become our behavior and we are no longer imposters. We become what we visualize for ourselves.

If you don't believe that this works, let me introduce you to Frank Abagnole. Before Frank was even 25 years old, he had successfully passed himself off as an airline pilot and a doctor. His story was captured in the book and movie, <u>Catch Me if You Can</u>. Abagnale had actual professional airline pilots convinced he was a pilot and professional physicians convinced he was a doctor. He acted the part until he became it. Everyone believed him. Eventually he was caught and served some hard time. But now he helps government and corporations prevent fraud, protecting them from the very things that he was getting away with.

Like Abagnale, if you work on the vision you have for yourself, you not only become it, but it becomes you. Own that vision and become that person, all day, every day. You *are* the writer, you *are* the successful entrepreneur, you *are* the CEO. Whatever it is, when you get to that point, you've taken possession of your target in your mind and you've earned it. You now *know* that this is who you are.

Certainly, it helps if you are competent, courageous and resolute as you take on this identity. You may need some training and education along with your acting ability. But you can get those things *while* you assume your new identity.

Still not sure?

Once upon a time there was a young working-class British actor named Archie Leach. Archie used the very process we are outlining to become Cary Grant. He decided that he would act like a high-class aristocrat and eventually, everyone saw him as one. He took possession of who he was in his mind and everyone else bought in as well.

This has worked for me also. People that know me are surprised to find out that on personality inventories, I test out as an introvert. They typically see me as a speaker or musician out in front of large crowds, or even occasionally being the life of the party. But truly, it's not my nature. I've learned how to take on the role of a speaker and entertainer and I've become those roles. This absolutely works.

I've also been fortunate to belong to a few elite social clubs in the Seattle area. As a result, I find myself at an occasional party or networking event where I know very few people. But rather than succumb to my own shy nature, I've learned a trick that works every time. I pretend that I'm the host of the event. Seriously! People will come in and I'll ask if I can grab them a drink or hang their coat. I'll point out where things are and simply pretend that it's my event. Not only do I get comfortable but I make others comfortable and make them feel welcome as well. It never detracts from the event and it forces me to get into my "extrovert" role, which once I get rolling, I typically play quite well.

Some people argue that assuming this identity makes me a phony. Not at all. How is this person not me? It's simply me actualizing another part of myself. And I like to think of it as me at my best. Why would I not want to bring my best energy to a situation?

One final note about visualization: To some extent, we are always visualizing whether we are aware of it or not. So it's important to reiterate that if imagining ourselves as a success leads to a great outcome, imagining fear and failure can lead to a poor one. It's fine to imagine ourselves facing adversity and to see ourselves overcoming it. But it's useful to remember that it's the emotional weight of our imagination that causes many of our problems. So we must vigilantly challenge any thoughts and pictures that our minds run that are not conducive to success. How do we learn to do that?

We meditate.

Tool 5: Meditation

If we hope to go anywhere or develop ourselves in any way, we can only step from where we are standing. If we don't really know where we are standing...we may only go in circles.

- Jon Kabat-Zinn

What does meditation have to do with mental toughness?

Very simply, everything. Meditation occurs whenever we pay attention to the unfolding of the present moment in all its fullness. When we attend to something fully, we see possibilities that might not have been evident before. Meditation trains us to become more aware of our thoughts, both the useful and not-so-useful. This enables us to see things more clearly and to examine our own knee-jerk reactivity. Most importantly, it is the first step in learning just where our attention is – which opens up the potential for us to place it wherever we want it to go. We can't be mentally tough if our thoughts are jumping from one thing to the next like monkeys on trees. However, once we can take charge of our minds, there is very little we cannot accomplish.

When meditating, we watch our thoughts as they pass through. I often think of these thoughts as clouds passing through the sky. We don't judge them, we just observe them. Once we've practiced meditation for a few weeks or months, we also begin to notice our thoughts in everyday life. We bring that same "noticing" into the world. We begin to notice patterns in our thinking. We begin to understand that we think many of the same thoughts, day after day. In fact, it's been estimated that we think between sixty and seventy-thousand thoughts per day. Between eighty and ninety percent of those are the same thoughts as the day before.

As we continue our meditation practice, we begin to realize that a number of our thoughts do not serve our greater good. They do not help us to hit our targets. Many of our sixty-thousand thoughts are worries and judgments. "Am I making as much money as my colleague? Am I too fat? Does the boss hate me? I hope my car doesn't die on the way home; it's been sounding funny. Was I supposed to stop at the store?"

At this point, our minds are jumping from one thought to the next. Almost none of these thoughts are helping us to implement our offensive mindset. Remember that first proactive question of the day, *"What am I going to get done?"*

Meditation trains us to become more aware. Awareness leads to more informed and deliberate choices. And an informed and deliberate choice is not often the easiest one. That's why learning to choose where to put our attention enhances our mental toughness.

Our mind goes where our attention flows. And because meditation helps us to direct our attention, a word about "distraction" is in order. Typically, we avoid distraction because it takes our focus away from our target. However, at times, deliberately moving our attention away from certain things can also be useful. For example, as an athlete, there have been many times I've had to lose weight for a competition. I've found myself becoming almost obsessed with food. Meditation has allowed me to become aware of when that obsession is occurring. Recognizing that, I can choose how I want to deal with it. Distraction is sometimes the best choice.

We can deliberately distract ourselves when it serves our greater good. In this way, it becomes yet another informed choice. If I'm trying to make weight for a competition, I will get up and move when I begin thinking about food that's not on my schedule. Being productively busy, both mentally and physically, can take your mind away from your hunger.

If I've suffered a loss, whether in sports, my profession, or a relationship, rather than obsess about the defeat, I will distract myself by working to improve myself. It might be a trip to the gym or a trip to the bookstore but in any case, I get motivated to get better. Using distraction in this manner actually refocuses you onto the very thing in which you wish to excel. You're not running away from your problem, but you're using distraction to put your mind on a more productive activity.

The awareness you gain in meditation helps you to realize when your mind has abandoned the offensive mindset in favor of reactive, fear-based thinking. It then allows you to make choices and to use your mind and body in constructive ways.

The Science Behind Meditation

It is now impossible to ignore the benefits of meditation. Using magnetic resonance imaging (MRI) and other brain scanning capabilities, neuroscientists can peer directly into the brain to see what's happening. In addition to numerous anecdotal studies touting the advantages, there are now a number of scientific ones as well. Health-related advantages seem to crop up the most.

One such study was published in a 2012 edition of the journal, *Circulation: Cardiovascular Quality and Outcomes*. This study looked at 201 people with coronary heart disease. Each individual was asked to either 1) take a health education class that advocated better nutrition and exercise or 2) take a transcendental meditation course. Follow-ups over a five year period showed that those who took the meditation class had a 48% greater reduction in their risk of heart attack, stroke and death. Other heart-related studies demonstrate how meditation slows breathing and pulse rates, in addition to lowering blood pressure.

Then there are those who suffer from chronic pain. Mindfulness meditation helps those people step back and observe how they're labeling their pain as intolerable when in fact, they are indeed tolerating it in their present moment. It's the idea that they'll have to live with it forever that makes them suffer. Understanding that right now they are coping helps them to get away from looking into a future that they cannot actually predict. They begin to see how the emotion they attach to their pain increases their suffering. That's not to say that the pain isn't there, it absolutely is. But meditation gives them an awareness of how they're handling it and some options as to how they might deal with it in future present moments.

Perhaps most interesting is the scientific finding that meditation actually changes the brain's structure. A 2005 Harvard study looked at 20 people who regularly meditated and 20 who did not. The results were dramatic. Areas within the cortex of the brain related to attention, sensory awareness and emotional processing were thicker in those who meditated. Additionally, it seemed brains grew thicker relative to how much the subjects actually meditated.

Another 2012 study amplified this finding. This study demonstrated that those who meditate have higher levels of what's called gyrification. This gyrification is a "folding" of the cerebral cortex due to growth. While not proven directly, scientists suspect that this cortical growth allows the brain to process information more rapidly. They also believe that there would likely be improved cognitive, emotional and immune responses tied to this growth.

Other studies have shown that in just eight weeks, meditation will decrease the production of the stress hormone, cortisol. This typically helps people function in higher stress situations and when practiced before a stressful event, meditation can help with focus and mental agility.

How to Meditate

There are numerous traditions and different methods of meditation. There is a tremendous amount of information on everything from Zen to Transcendental Meditation on-line as well as in your local library. I practice "mindfulness meditation" and I'll briefly address that here.

Meditation does not have to be some mystical, esoteric experience. The most difficult part for most people is simply sitting quietly. It has become even more difficult in recent years as we have become more addicted to having constant information coming in through our phones and computers.

It helps to have a sense of humor because as you begin to watch your thoughts, you realize that they're all over the map. Most of us begin to realize, "Oh good heavens, I'm a lunatic!"

That's why a sense of humor helps. If we can laugh at ourselves when we catch ourselves going off on some train of thought, we can more quickly regain control of our thinking and put our attention on simply observing the present moment. Once we become skilled in doing that, then we can harness our thoughts to place them on what we're going to do right now. And right now is where life is lived. The present is always right now. The past and future exist only in our imagination.

If you are just beginning a meditation practice, I recommend sitting for five minutes. If you are a typical member of this go-go-go culture, sitting and doing nothing for five minutes will be very difficult. You will get restless. You will wonder about the emails and texts you may be missing. Sitting will seem like a waste of time. In fact, it is anything but.

I recommend getting into a comfortable seated position with your back straight and feet on the floor. You don't need a "meditation cushion" and you don't need to cup your hands in some esoteric "mudra position" to be effective. Your hands will be fine resting on your thighs or on the arms of your chair.

Relax and concentrate on your breath. It might be useful to count breaths. Immediately, you will find how difficult it is to even count down from five breaths before other thoughts intervene. This is fine and normal. Just notice your thoughts without judging them or yourself for having them. Then bring your mind back to your breath. Just listen. What do you notice? What do you hear? Feel your toes. Notice them. If you are uncomfortable, just notice the discomfort without judging it as awful. Then go back to concentrating on your breath.

After you get comfortable sitting for five minutes, and you will, try 10. Later, move to fifteen or 20 minute sessions. You'll notice your thinking as you sit and you'll watch your mind like an observer. Once you can do that, you begin to notice your mind and what you're thinking as you go about your everyday activities.

Paying attention and noticing your mind is the first step towards directing it towards what you want to get done. While you are meditating, you are continually bringing your mind back to your breath. You are learning how to focus. Meditation allows you to master your mind because it gives you the facility to corral your thoughts and place your mind wherever you want it to be. This takes us right back to our offensive mindset. *"What am I going to get done?"*

When you begin your meditation practice, it's useful to be able to do it in a quiet setting at a consistent time every day. Eventually, as your practice deepens, you'll be able to do it in a crowded and noisy airport. The idea isn't to block out the noise; the idea is to notice it, not judge it, and bring yourself back to your breath. This helps you learn how to focus through chaos, an incredible skill to have.

I've always thought of meditation as my own form of strength training for the brain. The ability to watch your mind, pay attention and focus your thoughts makes you incredibly powerful. You can notice and rid yourself of thoughts that do not lead to your targets. Meditation is truly the foundation of mental toughness because it puts you in charge of you!

If we can agree that mental toughness is enhanced by greater focus, concentration and clarity, meditation is a must. Meditation also helps us to learn and practice yet another mental toughness tool that we will explore next.

Tool 6: Deep Breathing

"If you don't think that breathing is the most important thing you can do, try not doing it."

- Lee Witt

Sometimes the most useful mental toughness tools are the simplest and easiest to access. Breathing is the body's most important task simply because every other bodily function depends on it. The oxygen we breathe is required for survival. Our breathing also allows us to remove waste and toxins from the body. We can go for weeks without food but without oxygen, we'll only last a few minutes.

We cannot think or perform optimally without the kind of oxygen that only deep breathing can supply. In addition, going back to our breath grounds us. It is the most basic element that will put us in touch with the present moment, which is where everything happens.

Typically, under stress, we begin to breathe rapidly and shallowly. This wastes energy and keeps us from expelling the stale air from our lungs. This stale air can be toxic and lead to sluggishness. In addition, rapid, shallow, chest breathing keeps us from optimally delivering nutrients to our tissues. On the other hand, deep breathing from the abdomen (or diaphragm) slows our heart rate and brings our nervous system back into balance. When we are feeling stressed, deep, controlled breathing will balance our body and mind, which leads to better decision making.

When possible, the nose should be our primary organ for breathing. Nose breathing stimulates our parasympathetic nervous systems. This breathing suppresses a fear response that comes when we activate our sympathetic nervous system. Our sympathetic nervous system regulates our heart rate, blood pressure, circulation and other bodily functions. Certainly, when engaged in vigorous physical activity, we'll be using both our mouth and nose to take in oxygen. But in the normal course of our daily activity, deep nose breathing will keep us healthier.

You can use your meditation sessions to practice deep breathing. I have found that breathing in to a count of three and out to a count of 5 or 6will allow about 6 to 7 breaths per minute. At that rate, we both slow our heart rate and bring our blood pressure down as well.

Some people prefer to perform what is often called "box breathing" or "square breathing." An example of this would be to 1) breathe in to a count of four; 2) hold the breath to a count of four; 3) exhale to a count of four and 4) wait to a count of four before breathing again. You can increase the count to five, six or whatever works for you. The key is to use the same count for each of the four process steps.

It is this slowing down process that makes focusing on the breath so valuable during a crisis or time when you become paralyzed with fear. If you're feeling panicky, your mind is generally out of control and having several conversations at once. Or it may become fixated on one single sentence such as, "I'm going to die." Focusing on a deep breath brings you back and grounds you to the present moment. It creates just enough space for a clear thought to emerge. This clarity of thought can then lead you to an effective strategy and action.

When things get chaotic, our thoughts can become like a rapidly raging river, completely out of control. Our challenge is to slow down and witness these thoughts, manage them, and direct them. If we don't, it will be incredibly difficult, if not impossible to move through and beyond our panic.

Slowing down our thinking by using the breath will allow us to focus on the one thing that matters. And that thing is typically the action we need to take that is right in front of us. We can move forward from that place.

The most mentally tough people are the ones who can take charge of their moments. Taking charge of your breath is the quickest way to begin that process. Deep, slow breathing is the tool that will allow you to access your best thinking, your best energy, and your best outcomes.

Tool 7: Power Posing

"You want to feel that you have the power to bring your full, spirited self to the situation, stripped of the fears and inhibitions that might typically hold you back."

- Amy Cuddy

Approximately twenty-five years ago, self-help coach Tony Robbins was talking about physiology and its effect on performance. He didn't have scientific data but he knew from experience that if you stood tall and acted strong and magnificent, you would have a better chance of actually *being* strong and magnificent. We had only to watch a proud bullfighter adopt the "matador walk" to provide anecdotal evidence that posture can enhance courage. For years, athletes, professional dancers, and people who made a living off of their physicality knew this intuitively and experientially.

Now, thanks to Harvard researcher Amy Cuddy and her colleagues, we have the scientific data to support this. Dr. Cuddy has shown how changes in our body language can actually change our body chemistry. Using what she calls "power poses," we can significantly and positively affect our mental toughness and performance. This is particularly noteworthy because it isn't just about how others perceive us; it's about how we perceive ourselves.

Many of us, at times, have probably felt that our minds and bodies were fighting with one another. As we know, the body sometimes craves things that the mind knows isn't good for it.

As we consider this struggle between mind and body, it can be useful to think of ourselves as a triad. We have a mind, a body, and yet there is something else. That something else is that third part of us that can watch and witness both the mind and body as they battle. We will call this part of ourselves, *the observer*.

The skills of the observer are greatly enhanced through one of our previous tools, the practice of meditation. The observer notices and becomes aware of what is going on. It then holds those observations in its awareness long enough to make a conscious decision on how to act. This is a key component in the idea of mind over matter. Once aware, the observer can direct the mind on the best course of action, and the mind can instruct the body on what to do.

Too often however, we allow the body to be in charge and its influence over the mind can be dramatic. However, with Dr. Cuddy's research, we now know that we can exploit this. We can use the body's influence over our minds to our benefit!

We need only look at the animal kingdom to find that within many different species, expansive and open postures generally result in the perception of power and dominance. On the other hand, withdrawn, closed, and contracted postures are more likely to result in the perception of powerlessness.

It's the same for humans. And as it turns out, these different postures have neurochemical correlations. Expansive, dominant postures are correlated with higher levels of testosterone. Testosterone is a hormone linked with dominance and confidence. These expansive postures also correlate with lower levels of cortisol, a hormone associated with stress. Conversely, more closed and contracted postures are correlated with low testosterone and high cortisol.

For many years, scientists believed that it was our inherited traits that predicted socially dominant behaviors. Dr. Cuddy's research proved that the opposite was also possible, that is; *if we act powerfully, our bodies assume the neurochemistry of power*. She and her colleagues experimented with 42 male and female volunteers. They began by measuring the baseline hormone levels of each subject.

Once hormone levels were established, each individual was told to assume high-power or low-power poses for two minutes. A high-power pose was characterized by openness with the body being spread out to take up a good deal of space. Arms could be uplifted in the same manner as one who had just won a race or sank a 30-foot putt. We often call this "the victory position." Or people could stand like they imagined Superman or Wonder Woman would, confident, hands on hips, open and in charge.

Contrarily, a low-power pose was characterized by being bent over as if texting on a phone or physically contracting to take up less space. Imagine sitting on a couch with your knees drawn up and hugging yourself with both arms. That's a low power posture.

After 17 minutes, the subjects' hormones were measured again. The results were remarkable. The testosterone levels for the high-power posers shot up by as much as 20%. Cortisol dropped by 25%. Participants also reported having feelings of increased power and a greater tolerance for risk. So while we know that our minds can change our bodies, it seems that our bodies can also change our minds.

Smiling Makes a Difference!

Even a forced smile can make a huge difference. In a 1988 study, subjects were told to hold a pencil between their teeth that forced them to smile. They did this while performing a task that involved rating the degree of humor in cartoons. Other participants were told to hold the pencil between their lips without touching the pencil with their teeth. This forced the muscles in their faces to contract into a frown. Afterwards, the subjects who were forced to smile judged the cartoons to be significantly funnier than those forced to frown.

Since then, this experiment has been duplicated in a variety of ways. In 2011, pencils were replaced by chopsticks in order to manipulate the facial muscles of 169 subjects into a 1) neutral expression, 2) a standard smile, or 3) a Duchenne smile . A Duchenne smile fully engages the face to the point where there is crinkling around the eyes. While keeping the chopsticks in their mouths, the participants were subjected to a series of stress-inducing activities. Their heart rates and self-reported stress levels were monitored throughout.

The smiling subjects were reported to have lower heart rates and those with the Duchenne smiles were the most relaxed of all. So having a forced smile induced by chopsticks makes you feel better than not smiling at all.

So what can we take from this? Plenty. When it's time to deliver, we can use our bodies to put ourselves into a high-performance state. Something as simple as an open, spread-out posture and a forced smile can decrease our stress and increase our feelings of confidence and dominance.

I find myself performing these actions in the weight room when I'm experiencing profound muscular fatigue. The natural tendency is to bend over at the waist and contract the body. But with more sets yet to do, I'll stand up, stretch out wide and put a big smile on my face. In as little as 5 to 10 seconds, I can feel more energy. Even in the midst of a set, I'll force a smile, as if I've got those chopsticks forced into my face. It truly makes a difference, and it is one more competitive advantage that I use.

In addition to the biochemical benefits of smiling, you get the bonus of:

1) Being more attractive to others;
2) Having a positive contagious effect on others who smile back;
3) A lowered blood pressure; and
4) A release of endorphins and serotonin, natural pain relievers.

I've now adopted power posing as a regular part of my routine. I also smile and assume a power pose before a speech, presentation or musical performance. Sometimes I'll walk in an exaggeratedly proud manner like the Spanish matadors. (Typically, I prefer to do this alone in a room where people won't think I'm insane.) As I do it, I can almost feel my testosterone going up and my cortisol levels dropping. My energy is greater and I'm conscious of bringing my best self to the moment. And really, that's what it's all about. As Amy Cuddy suggests, why wouldn't we want to increase the number of times we bring our best selves to the situations in our lives?

The bottom line? When we deliberately engage our minds and bodies, our mental toughness skyrockets.

Tool 8: Impulse Control

"You must get comfortable being uncomfortable."

- Tim Grover

Initially, I called this tool "Willpower" because I still believe in the power of the human will and spirit. I believe in it because I've exercised my own willpower to transcend several of my own personal genetic limitations. However, there has been a lot of research attempting to justify why willpower isn't enough. The research and studies are interesting in attempting to prove that willpower is a limited resource and we'll look at those studies. But in my mind they don't tell the whole story. Limited does not mean completely gone. It simply means limited.

To my way of thinking, the studies give no credence to the human spirit. Instead, they provide excuses and justifications for people who want to rationalize why they can't lose weight, beat addictions, or succeed in general. Because we love excuses, studies like these, and the books promoting them, sell. We love having a built-in excuse because then we don't have to be accountable for our failures. However, there is one positive thing coming from these studies. These studies advocate for having a strategy that will help us avoid the "low willpower" moments. That's a very useful idea. And yes, *we all have low willpower moments.*

As a result of the scientific community's questions around control of our own willpower, I changed the name of this tool. I selected a concept that is very agreeable to the scientific community. Even the experts saying that willpower isn't enough agree that what we call "impulse control" is an immensely important ingredient of success. When combined with intelligence, impulse control is said to be the greatest predictor of a successful and satisfying life. It is a central component of the human will and an absolute must for those looking to master mental toughness.

We exercise impulse control every time we eat vegetables when we crave a greasy hamburger. We exercise impulse control whenever we stop ourselves from making an unkind comment that would feel good in the moment but create long term ill will. We exercise impulse control whenever we turn off the television to go exercise.

According to research, the average human spends three to four hours per day resisting desires and cravings. In addition, impulse control is also used to control thoughts and emotions, make decisions and regulate task performance. This means that we are using our impulse control and willpower several times a day. And as we'll see when we look at the science, this leads to those low willpower moments.

The key to impulse control and willpower is really the secret sauce behind everything in this book. It is the simplest concept we could ever invent. And it really just comes down to this one idea: WE HAVE TO WANT WHAT WE WANT VERY BADLY. *And we have to remain conscious of that want all of the time.*

The iconic 19th century poet, philosopher and critic, Friedrich Nietzsche, said, "He who has a why can bear with any how." Nietzsche was simply saying that if your reason for doing something is compelling enough, you will work to overcome any obstacles standing in your way.

What Nietzsche said still holds true. If greatness is our target, we have to want to be great more than we want comfort and ease. We have to want to be great more than we want to be at happy hour. We have to want to be great more than we want to hit the snooze alarm. We have to want to be great more than we want that dessert we are craving. And we have to want to be great more than we want to give up because we're tired.

This requires serious motivation and a burning desire to be more in every present moment. Otherwise, it's just too easy to put off things like good nutrition until tomorrow. It's too easy to listen to friends and family saying, "Oh, just this once won't hurt." It's too easy to put off exercise until Monday. It's too easy to put off the important office work that is waiting for you. It's too easy to give in to every form of sabotage that exists.

Yes, in order to be great, we have to want it. And it's never easy. It's simple, but not easy. That's why greatness is rare. And there is inherent risk because there is no guarantee that we will eventually succeed in what we attempt. But I guarantee that we won't succeed if we don't show up and go for it. And it will occasionally hurt. As such, we must be unreasonable and relentless when we pursue greatness. Embracing the suck must become an afterthought to the point where we hardly even notice we're uncomfortable. The discomfort is just built in to the formula.

Winning the Treadmill Test

The treadmill test is actually an idea and metaphor that entertainer Will Smith popularized. Saying that he has a ridiculous and absolutely sick work ethic, Smith credits hard work more than talent for his own success. I have always embraced that same idea, and the treadmill test provides a wonderful metaphor to help people understand the discipline involved. Having this kind of work ethic requires immense impulse control and what pop psychologists now refer to as "grit."

In essence, the treadmill test boils down to the following passage:

You may be bigger than me. You may be faster than me. You may be stronger than me. You may be smarter than me. You may be more talented than me. And you may be better looking than me, but I will tell you one thing: If you and I get on a treadmill, one of two things is going to happen. You're going to get off first – or I'm going to die.

I love that!

I am not afraid to die on a treadmill. This means that I might get beat but I will not be outworked or outhustled. I will recover every fumble. I will grab every rebound and dive after every loose ball. I will read and return every email. I will listen to and respond to every voice mail. I will not be outworked because how hard I work is under my control.

Now, as an intelligent human being, you may be thinking that this sounds horrible. Why would anyone allow themselves to die, metaphorically or not, on a treadmill?

Here's why. *Because you're going to die anyway.* Wouldn't you rather live leaving it all on the playing field? Wouldn't you rather use the time you have going after something big? Only you can decide what that is. Only you can decide your own path to greatness.

Taking on this attitude has allowed me to transcend a limited heritage and approach the upper limits of my genetic potential both physically and mentally. It has enabled me to produce at a level far beyond others who are substantially more gifted than me. If you're 60 years old and you've been playing small all of your life, you can still play big. You can still choose greatness.

When we add impulse control to this desire to be great, we have immense power. Impulse control enables us to choose the harder right instead of the easier wrong. It requires present moment awareness. It requires sacrifice. In fact, all of the tools we have outlined to this point are designed to enhance impulse control. How so?

Tool 1: Our offensive mindset propels us towards action and provides the foundation for the "want to be great."

Tools 2, 3 and 4: Our agenda, plan, instructional self-talk and visualization tools provide us with the steps we need to take.

Tool 5: Meditation reinforces present moment awareness that enables us to recognize when we are about to make an impulse-driven choice.

Tool 6: Deep breathing slows us down so that we can consider our choices when we feel the stress of a difficult challenge or decision.

Tool 7: Power posing gives us the opportunity to express physical courage and to take on the biochemistry required to reinforce greatness and exercise impulse control.

Each tool to this point leads to making the decisions that bring us closer to our targets. As we consider the tool of impulse control, let's look at some of the recent research and what it says about human willpower. Again, the value of the research is that it encourages us to have a strategy that enables us to maximize our willpower before it runs low.

The Science Behind Willpower and Impulse Control

Roy Baumeister, a social psychologist at Florida State University, was the first to suggest that willpower was indeed a limited resource. Baumeister's 1998 studied implied that drawing on a supply of self-control and willpower in one instance will deplete that person's ability to use it subsequently. In other words, it seems that repeated temptations take a mental toll. How so?

Baumeister brought test subjects into a room. On a table in front of them sat a big plate of freshly-baked cookies. Next to the cookies was a bowl of radishes. Some subjects were told that it was okay to eat the cookies. Others were told that they could only eat the radishes. All were then given a half-hour to complete an unsolvable geometric puzzle. Those who had been asked to resist the cookies and eat the radishes quit, on average, after about eight minutes. Those who ate the cookies kept on for an average of 19 minutes before giving up. It seems that those who had to exercise self-control (radish eaters) had less willpower to apply to the puzzle.

This also suggests that glucose (blood sugar) may play a role in impulse control. Our brains require energy that comes from a steady stream of glucose. If brain cells are working diligently to exercise willpower, they may in fact consume glucose supplies faster than they can be restocked. This has now been born out in the laboratory. Tests have shown that people forced to exert willpower had lower blood sugar amounts than those not required to exercise impulse control. Other tests have shown that having lowered glucose levels not only depletes our willpower, but also increases our propensity towards anger and violence.

If this is true, it makes sense to believe that restoring glucose levels to depleted people would recharge their willpower batteries. To test this simple idea, one experimenter gave sugar-sweetened lemonade to subjects who were glucose-depleted. This did in fact restore willpower strength to those individuals. People given sugar-free lemonade showed no such restoration of willpower. A victory for glucose.

Since Baumeister conducted his studies, numerous follow-on studies have continued to make a case for how willpower gets depleted. In one such study, subjects were asked to watch an emotional movie and to suppress their feelings about it. Afterwards, they gave up much sooner on a test of physical stamina than those who were allowed to react normally to the same movie. A similar study asked people to suppress certain thoughts and they were less able to stifle laughter in a follow-up test devised to make them giggle.

Having a Strategy

Recently, researchers at the University of Toronto also helped to verify Baumeister's findings. They discovered that our brains actually function differently when our willpower has been tested. After giving people a series of tasks requiring self-control, subjects showed decreased activity in the anterior cingulate cortex, a brain area engaged in cognition. So the evidence is compelling that there are actual physical reasons for failing to exercise impulse control.

Of course, who among us hasn't reached for a feel-good sugar snack when we were tired? Who among us hasn't failed to follow through on some form of self-denial after having had to make a number of difficult decisions? And it doesn't require a lab experiment to know that hungry, tired people sometimes get cranky. As a result, scientists suggest that we develop strategies to keep our blood sugar elevated and stable if we are going to have a difficult discussion with a loved one, or a day-long battle of decision making at work. Having healthy food available is one simple way of keeping ourselves steady and in control of our impulses.

It also helps to have the kind of self-awareness that comes with our fifth mental toughness tool, meditation. The practice of meditation will keep us mindful of our choices in the midst of a difficult moment. Knowing when we're about to experience a lapse in impulse control is the first step towards making an informed decision.

Happily, there is evidence indicating that we can improve our self-control at any age. Like our muscles, our self-control gets stronger with exercise. Creating a strategy to practice self-control activities for even a few weeks improves our ability to control our impulses. This is true even on things that have no relation to the exercise activities. The exercises can be random, such as using our non-dominant hand to operate a computer mouse or brush our teeth. Or they can be significant, such as controlling our spending and saving money. Even mindfully practicing good posture strengthens our "impulse control" muscles.

The main thing is to practice different ways of performing our habitual activities and to apply deliberate control over our behavior. Over time, this improves our self-control.

Beyond the Science: The Battle Override

While I don't discount the research we've examined, I believe it severely underestimates human potential. Yes, exerting our will and controlling our impulses are difficult and demanding exercises. Fatigue, blood sugar levels, and lower cognitive activity all make self-control much more challenging. But challenging is not the same as impossible.

I believe that the research is being used by some as another way to normalize limitations. If we buy into the belief that we only have a certain amount of control over our impulses, we set ourselves up to fall short. If all of the people who have ever achieved anything significant believed that they could only exert a certain amount of willpower before they gave up, we'd be driving around in covered wagons.

In 2010, Dr. Veronika Job, a Stanford University researcher, tested people and found that those who believed that willpower was a limited resource were apt to actualize that belief. Conversely, those who did not buy in to the idea that their impulse control muscles were easily exhaustible showed no signs of willpower depletion. She also found that people in good moods were more able to resist temptation than their crankier counterparts.

I cannot imagine telling a Navy SEAL who survived hell week that he doesn't have the ability to control his impulse to quit. Really? After all, he *did* control his impulse to quit. Navy SEALs and those who achieve great things by working through discomfort employ what I call the *"battle override."* The battle override is like a switch you throw once you recognize that you're in extreme discomfort. Upon throwing that switch, you don't care about anything but hitting your target. Once you've switched on, you can override your blood glucose level. You can override your crankiness. You can override pain. Thousands of people have and I am one of them.

As athletes will often say, "You can't measure the size of a person's heart." I believe this is true. A person's desire to hit a target can be far greater than temporary or even severe discomfort. It can be greater than a difficult addiction. Otherwise, people couldn't quit cigarettes, caffeine and other even more insidious drugs cold turkey. *If one person has been able to do it, that proves that it's humanly possible.*

We have become very excuse-prone as a society. When things get hard, we give up. We then find a variety of excuses, justifications and rationalizations as to why.

One of the most useful things to understand is that we only have to control our impulse in this moment. We don't have to control it later, just now. When later becomes now, we can control it then as well. Staying in the present is a terrific strategy for controlling your impulses. It absolutely works.

But once again, it all boils down to that secret sauce. *We have to want what we want very badly.* Decide what you want, employ the battle override – and go!

Tool 9: Perspective, References and Crucible Experiences

"The losses of age are greatly exaggerated."

- Pat Jordan

Everything is relative, right?

All of us have had numerous life challenges. They vary in difficulty depending on the kind of lives we have led. Many of these challenges offer us a reference point for a time when we rose up to a difficulty and overcame it. Former Navy SEAL commander Mark Divine calls these moments, "crucible experiences."

A crucible experience provides you with a frame of reference that you can draw upon when things get tough. It reminds you that you've been through hard times and you've come through them. Anyone who has attained the age of 60 has surely surmounted a few formidable obstacles along the path.

For some it may have been completing a marathon, triathlon or adventure race. For others, it may have been enduring the trauma of chemotherapy. And still others may have suffered the vagaries of battle in wartime.

For those who have overcome immense challenge, the inconvenience of the Internet breaking down or the car not starting do not have the same impact. And while I do not recommend becoming a prisoner of war in order to heighten your perspective, I do recommend that you take whatever "your crucible experience" is and use it as a mental toughness reference point.

Someone I admire very much is James Webb. Webb is former Secretary of the Navy and also a former Virginia Senator. Furthermore, he is a Vietnam War veteran, renowned novelist and screenwriter. Webb's real life experiences allow him to speak of true heroism. He gives an example that very few of us can relate to, giving credence to the idea that "everything is relative."

Webb recounts the story of a military hero named John Paul Bobo. Bobo won a posthumous Medal of Honor because he got his leg blown off in battle, stuck his stump into the ground and continued fighting until he died.

Yes, you read that correctly. *He stuck his stump in the ground and continued to fight.*

Now, I like to think of myself as a tough guy but if I was ever to be separated from any of my limbs, there would be no stump-sticking and fighting on. I imagine that there would be a fair amount of screaming and cursing. But there would be no stump-sticking. The idea of fighting on while some of my body parts are residing in another zip code just does not resonate with me.

Bobo's experience is just one of numerous examples that give us a frame of reference from which we can compare our own troubles. Someone always has it worse. But I would encourage all of us to think back on our own "crucible experiences." These experiences give us the recognition and confidence that we can press forward when facing obstacles.

For myself, I think back to 84-hour work weeks in the hot Illinois summers at the Green Giant Company. Putting myself through college required it. Sometimes those work weeks grew to 94 hours if I was lucky enough to grab a piano bar job on the weekend.

I did this for three summers and have referred to these experiences throughout my adult life when I believed myself to be tired. For me, those summers taught me about fatigue and social deprivation. They also taught me the value of money and a college education. While hardly a wartime experience, there is very little in my daily life that is difficult relative to those years.

I was heartened to hear some time ago that requiring people to work those kinds of hours was no longer legal. But it wasn't just the work and the hours that made it difficult. It was that many of the people working with me were ex-cons, migrant workers and people of very limited education. They weren't too keen on a college boy in their midst. Every day was a test and a challenge; sometimes a physical one. No kind of bullying is acceptable, but when I hear all of the whining about "Internet bullying," it makes me shake my head. I would vastly prefer that compared to the 280 pound Texan just out of San Quentin that found me very attractive.

I encourage all of us to think back to a time when we endured something that seemed unendurable. Somehow, we found a way to persevere and make it through. It may not have been as heroic as what many legendary war heroes have endured; but it doesn't have to be. It just has to prove to us that we've had the right stuff in the past – and we can access that same mental toughness again.

Draw upon those experiences when times get tough. You've made it through before. You will again.

Gratitude

We would be remiss if we didn't mention gratitude as part of the "perspective" aspect of mental toughness. Gratitude is mentioned so often in the happiness literature that it's almost cliché. But gratitude is not simply the key to happiness; there is a mental toughness component that recognizes it as a toughness strategy.

The greatest philosophers and spiritual teachers from Cicero to Buddha to Christ have celebrated gratitude as the parent of all virtues. Grateful people are more enthusiastic, alert, determined, optimistic and energetic. That translates to mental toughness.

Grateful people experience less stress and depression. They are more likely to help others. They exercise more regularly and advance more readily towards personal goals. In addition, they report feeling loved more often and feel like their kindnesses are returned more readily. Again, this translates to mental toughness.

Experiencing gratitude is a choice and a practice. Eventually, it can become a skill. The practice of counting our blessings has always increased our personal well being. In addition, it has a positive impact on the environment. *If we can focus on what is right with our lives as opposed to what is wrong, this attitude will bring on a shift that can transform our entire existence.* This attitude is entirely up to us. It is a choice – and it translates to mental toughness.

When we feel lack, we suffer. Often, our feeling of lack stems from our inability to accept the world as it is. And of course, in a consumer-oriented society, we are trained to feel lack. But because we know that it's all made up, we know that our feeling of lack is made up as well. Our feeling of lack is simply a judgment. If you feel you're missing something, you've made it up. You are playing a mental game of comparison that is completely unnecessary.

The richest people on earth are the ones who appreciate what they have. No one who is grateful is unhappy. And this is not to suggest that you shouldn't go for more. By all means, kick absolute ass and create wealth. I'm simply suggesting that you not get hung up on what you don't have. Get hung up on what you DO have and go get more! Think of how much philanthropy you can perform with your abundance.

This entire book has been about being grateful for the amazing gift of life – and then using it to serve and succeed. *Think of the amazing blessings that are yours every day!* If you're a senior member of society, be grateful that you still have a pulse and a heartbeat. You're still in the game! If you have forgotten the amazing abundance that we live in, consider those that don't have enough food, shelter, or clothing. Our quality of life is unparalleled in the history of the world.

If I wake up in the morning and find myself complaining, I stop and ask myself, "Is there really anything to complain about?" Surely I am tougher than this. Am I in the middle of a war zone being bombed? No. So I get back to my offensive mindset and ask myself, "What am I going to get done?"

Why complain about our jobs? I am grateful to have gainful employment. Why complain about that? Even if the job sometimes requires embracing the suck, that's part of the deal. Every job does. That's why they call it "work." Many people are unemployed. I have the opportunity to contribute at work and to reap the rewards. And no one has a gun to my head forcing me to go to work every day. It's my decision. If I don't like it, I'm free to leave.

We can be grateful for the people we get to work with each day, even when they're difficult. Difficult people give us the opportunity to practice on how best to deal with them. How cool is that? Most likely, many of the people we work with have become friends. If we want to make more friends, we can serve someone. We can put out just a little extra energy. We can be grateful for the energy we have that gives us the opportunity to serve others. Serving others and thanking them is the most wonderful way to express our gratitude. *Gratitude and service are two sides of the same coin.* If we bring service to our world, we'll have more friends than we can count.

I am grateful for my senses; my sight, my hearing, my ability to taste and smell amazing food and the glorious pleasure that only touch can provide. I am grateful to medical technology for providing me vision when it was practically gone.

I am grateful for the educational opportunities that are still available to me. This includes the amazing literature that exists no further away than my library, bookstore or Internet connection.

I am grateful to live in a country where I have freedom and the opportunity to choose.

Tool 10: Strategic Emotional Detachment

"Feel your feelings, but control your emotions."

- Lee Witt

The other day, I had lunch with some colleagues. When the conversation began to center on where Kanye West and Kim Kardashian would honeymoon, I mentally checked out. I began to stare at my spoon. It was infinitely more fascinating. Let's face it, Kanye peaked with "Gold Digger" in 2005 and it's been downhill ever since. And Kim, well, Kim never had a peak.

Not one to waste time, I looked for a way to amuse myself. I decided to play a game. I began trying to move the spoon with my mind. With every fiber of my psychic energy, I attempted to will the spoon to move.

Nothing happened.

I then picked up the spoon in one hand. I mentally got angry with it and glared at it. With all the mental force I could muster, I silently commanded the spoon to bend.

Again, nothing.

So I decided that a different approach might be in order. I thought back to the New Age literature of the 80's and 90's and began to send the spoon loving thoughts of healing, care and kindness. I then silently and gently cajoled it to bend.

Nada. Zip. The obstinate, ungrateful spoon still would not bend. And after all of that loving emotion! What a waste. Couldn't it sense how much I cared?

As I continued playing my game, the conversation at the table was shifting to Bruce Jenner's potential gender transformation. This also held no interest for me so I shifted my attention back to my spoon. Much like Kanye in 2005, Bruce also peaked early. In fact, it was 1976. Bruce looked great on the Wheaties box. After that, well…

Meanwhile, back at the spoon. This time I took the spoon in both hands and to the shock and awe of those at the lunch table who had no clue as to what I was doing, I bent the spoon into the shape of a horseshoe.

What's the moral of the story?

No, it's not that I'm a 60 year-old badass spoon bender; although that has a nice ring to it. (Great name for a band: "Please welcome…Badass Spoon Bender!")

No, the moral is: In terms of the real world, *action trumps emotion.*

Whether I sent the spoon angry emotional thoughts, or loving emotional thoughts, the spoon didn't budge until I picked it up and developed a physical relationship with it.

Why is this important? In our story, the spoon represents reality. The spoon and reality are simply what they are. We can hate reality, love it, or want it to be different and yet, it doesn't care.

We often pour tons of emotional energy into a situation. We will ruminate about it, dwell on it, or fixate on it. But all of that emotion doesn't make a bit of difference. Reality just goes on its merry way.

If the spoon represents reality, how I felt and thought about it didn't matter. However, how I acted upon the spoon did. Action bent the spoon. Emotion did not.

Nothing happens until we develop a physical relationship with reality. Our emotions might give us the impetus to act, but beyond that, nothing. Now I've read several accounts of how thoughts are energy and that they can change matter and that quantum physics can show us how reality is affected by our thinking. That may well be true. But I couldn't get the damn spoon to bend by thinking about it. (Where is Uri Geller when you need him?)

Now I will admit, with practice, I've been able to "biofeedback" myself and bring my blood pressure and pulse rates down. But I would maintain that it's my brain and body working together within a physical relationship. I imagine it would be more difficult for me to "biofeedback" someone else without that physical relationship. I am not saying that it's impossible; it just hasn't been part of my personal experience.

My point is simply that so much of our emotion is wasted. And much of it is useless, the most notable exception being "controlled anger." Rage typically does damage, both to the recipient and the person venting the rage. However, controlled anger can be used as fuel for progress. A good strategic "chip on the shoulder" coming from righteous anger can be a terrific catalyst for positive change.

The other useful feature of anger is that it doesn't coexist well with fear. When we are truly angry, I mean seriously angry, we're not afraid. And while I don't recommend either anger or fear, I prefer anger to fear. Just be sure that the anger has a strategic purpose.

We too often get wrapped up and emotionally involved in an outcome that negatively impacts our moods, relationships and results. It usually involves some sort of judgment and non-acceptance. We label something as bad and figure that it shouldn't be happening. If we can simply observe our own labeling process, we can recognize what's really going on – and then either accept it or create a plan to physically engage reality and change it.

Doing this on a repeated basis means that we have to recognize our emotions as they arise. Then we can examine them, hold them in our awareness as we would during a meditation session, and then either strategically use the emotion to drive us forward – or detach from it because it's useless.

Strategic detachment from our emotions typically gets us out of problems and into solutions much more rapidly. That usually leads to better outcomes.

The Roller Coaster

Imagine two people sitting next to each other on a roller coaster. One is terrified. The other loves it and finds it exhilarating. The emotions are all happening in the mind. It's all made up. Whether a person is feeling fear or excitement generally has nothing to do with the actual mechanics of the ride.

The lesson? *Take charge of your mind. Don't let what's going on inside your head dictate how you see what's outside.* Both people on the roller coaster are living the exact same moment doing the exact same thing. But their experience is different because of what's going on in their minds. We can choose what's going on in our own minds accordingly.

Think back to your meditation sessions and how you "non-judgmentally" watched your thoughts. It's useful to bring that same mentality to what we witness in real time. While it's appropriate to judge in many instances, it's also useful to suspend that judgment until we are certain that we have "seen clearly." Jumping to conclusions and getting emotional about what we *think* we see can cause a lot of damage. Wrong assumptions and faulty thinking can ruin careers and relationships. Removing the judgment and emotion, at least initially, can lead us to more successful outcomes. It's truly the mentally tough way to proceed.

Handling Stress the Mentally Tough Way

We can think of stress as the space between how the world is and how we would like it to be. Many of us throw a lot of energy into trying to eliminate that space – or at least make it smaller.

When we need the world to be a certain way in order for us to feel okay, we suffer. The world will never always be the way that we want. Our unrealistic expectations can quickly lead us into deep unhappiness.

If people are nice to me, I'm having a good day. If
they're not, I'm not.
If I have enough money, I'm happy. If I don't, I'm sad.
If I keep my job, I'm happy, if not, I'm sad.
If my kids behave…
If I have a good relationship…
If I lose weight…

We have a million of these "ifs." Using the offensive
mindset and our cache of tools, we can often avoid
these "ifs." But no one in the world has things go their
way all the time.

When things aren't going our way, we often feel stress.
And when we're stressed, we are chemically
imbalanced. Stress hormones begin racing through our
system. You know the feeling. At that moment, it's like
being on drugs. And we would never, hopefully, make
an important decision when we're on drugs. Yet that's
exactly what we do when we're stressed. We lose
clarity in the moment. We are much more effective
when we remove the effects of stress before making a
decision. Optimally, we won't feel the stress in the first
place.

So how do we do that?

We do it by practicing strategic emotional detachment.
This requires a fair amount of awareness and practice
because it's only natural to feel personally and
emotionally involved in our own lives.

I'm not suggesting that we detach from our feelings. I'm suggesting that in order to practice strategic emotional detachment, we need to recognize our feelings and then step back from the resulting emotion. This gives us the space to stay engaged, see clearly, and ensure that we are strategic in our next move. In other words, it's fine to feel our feelings. But then, it's imperative that we control our subsequent emotions.

When I attempt to step back before succumbing to an unhelpful emotion, I do what Navy SEALS are taught when infiltrating enemy territory. After extracting from the helicopter, they sometimes practice the acronym, SLLS-B. It stands for stop, look, listen, shut-up and breathe. It slows everything down and brings things back into the present. When I do this, I can remember that I don't have to be personally and emotionally involved in what's happening. I can work towards a certain outcome, but my self-worth and happiness need not be on the line.

I continually have to remind myself that I am not responsible for what's going on in the world. But I am absolutely responsible for what's going on in my mind. And I am NOT my mind! If I was, I couldn't observe it like I do when meditating.

The nursing profession gives us a very useful example of strategic emotional detachment. Personality tests can often predict the nurses who will burn out and fail. The ones that fail are the ones that "need" their patients to recover. It's just a fact that some patients will die. And of course, all of the nurses care very deeply about their patients. But the ones who can resist being personally and emotionally involved, while staying caring and engaged, are the ones with long and successful careers. They acknowledge their feelings, but they do not let their emotions get the best of them.

Now that we've explored the 10 Tools of Mental Toughness, it's time to go even deeper. It's time to take a glimpse into the world of *"Mastery."*

CHAPTER FIVE – *The Ideal of Mastery*

"For a man or a nation to be truly strong, each must be able to stand utterly alone, able to meet and deal with life relying solely upon his own inner resources. There may be no crutch of any kind employed, for when a crutch is removed, although one may retain balance for a short time, to fall is inevitable."

- G. Gordon Liddy

I am fascinated by the concept of mastery. To approach mastery is to move towards the ultimate in mental toughness. What exactly is mastery? It means different things to different people. When some people think of a master, they picture some guru-like figure sitting in the lotus position atop a mountain. Others picture captains of industry ruling their empires, taking phone calls and giving directions. This segment of the book will be devoted to my thoughts and opinions on the subject and what it means to me.

I view mastery as a directional pursuit. It is never attained, but always strived for. I think of it as a practice of continuous, relentless improvement. We can always get better, no matter what area we are working in. And really, why would we not want to be more powerful at age 60 than when we were at forty. Wisdom and experience can be powerful ingredients in a recipe that also includes functional physical prowess. At 60, we already have experience. If we've been paying attention, we also have wisdom. And our physical ability can and should be continually cultivated until we can no longer function.

To attain mastery is to reach the highest level in any activity that our genetic potential allows. It is to approach the ideal. So how do we begin? Much like we need an agenda, target and plan to implement our offensive mindset, we need a mission, stand and purpose to attain mastery. Integral to our stand are the values we aim to hold – and those values must be clarified and understood.

To give you an example of what I'm suggesting, here are the values, mission, stand and purpose to which I aspire as of this writing.

VALUES: Health, Humor, Generosity, Intelligence, Beauty

MISSION: Become the absolute authority on mid-life mastery relative to health, fitness, and emotional well being - and model that for others. Become the acknowledged authority on mental toughness, particularly for seniors.

STAND: *I stand for health, humor, generosity, intelligence and beauty.*

PURPOSE: *To be a model of possibility for what can be achieved in mid-life and beyond, to attain self-mastery, and to make every room I enter a better room.*

As we examine the above statements, we will begin with values. Values provide the foundation for all of our conduct. They are reflected in our stand – and they are worth examining in some detail.

Our values are reflected in what we do. They show up in our decisions and behaviors. When our values are clear, decisions become easy to make in real time. For example, my number one value is health. Without optimal health, it's difficult to enjoy and actualize all of the other values we may hold dear. So for me, if I have to choose between a piece of cake and a plate of vegetables, I simply ask, "Which choice aligns with my values?" Obviously, the vegetables win. Not because they are the best tasting or the most glamorous. It's because they reflect my value of health.

Now if I say that my greatest value is health, but I almost always choose the cake, in reality, health is not my greatest value. I may believe that it is, but my behavior suggests otherwise. The things that are important to us are the things that we do. *Those* are our values.

If I have to choose between working out and going to happy hour, I'm going to work out. That's what I do. That's who I am – and it reflects my value of health.

Please understand, I do not expect your values to be the same as mine. I'm simply referencing my own values to provide useful examples.

Here are some questions you can consider when clarifying your own values:

1) Who do I want to be?
2) What do I want to be?
3) If asked, what would I tell people is most important to me? Is that reflected in my actions?
4) How do I currently spend my time?
5) What do I believe is the best and greatest use of my time?

Whether they involve your children and family, your relationship with your God, money or career, your values are your own. If you're not clear on what they are, record your activities for a week and you'll find out relatively quickly what's most important to you. Then, if you're not happy with what you find out, you are free to change. You can act in accordance with your values and your new set of priorities. These will be the things you stand for – and you can begin to live by design and not by default.

Here is a list of potential values that may help you begin thinking about the concept. It is by no means comprehensive, but might give you some ideas.

Abundance, Accomplishment, Adventure, Art, Audacity, Belonging, Bravery, Calmness, Celebrity, Cleverness, Competence, Curiosity, Discipline, Education, Environmentalism, Excitement, Family, Fitness, Friendship, Fun, Gratitude, , Happiness, Independence, Individuality, Leadership, Mindfulness, Originality, Patience, Passion, Perseverance, Resilience, Reverence, Serenity, Spirituality, Strength, Success, Thoughtfulness, Tolerance, Truth, Unflappability, Valor, Vitality, Volunteerism, Warmth, Wisdom, Youthfulness, Zeal.

Whatever values you choose are yours. They may change over time. But you will find that many decisions become easier to make when you know what you stand for.

Consistency

Consistency is another prime indicator of what our values are. Our values reflect the actions we take *regardless* of what other people do. For example, in my own life, I make every effort to:

1) Make a **healthy** choice even when surrounded by peers who will not – and I do not succumb to any peer pressure to choose differently.

2) Find **humor** in a dire circumstance (often known as gallows humor). *Remember to embrace the suck!*
3) Be **generous** with my time, money and resources even when, or especially when, I think times are really tight. ("Hey Lee, put a crowbar in your wallet and pick up the tab for Christ's sake!")
4) Come up with an **intelligent** response under pressure when others seem to be panicking.
5) Find the **beauty** in whatever problem I am in the midst of, or perhaps create some.

While seemingly shallow on the surface, beauty is a value that we underestimate at our peril. One of the most poignant stories of why beauty is important comes from an extraordinary young man named Eric Greitans. Eric is a former U.S. Navy SEAL and Rhodes Scholar who has performed incredible humanitarian works all around the world.

Eric tells the story of a time he was in Bolivia. He was volunteering at a school for children who lived in desperate poverty. The few who actually had homes were typically abused and their futures seemed hopeless.

Eric was surprised that the school's proprietor spent so much time teaching art, music, painting, sculpture and dance. He suggested that perhaps reading, writing and math might be more practical. The proprietor explained that it was more important for the children to learn that, in the midst of their horrible conditions, there was still beauty in the world. Furthermore, they needed to understand that they could create it. Reading, writing and math were not going to give them what their souls needed.

This produced a truly different perspective for Eric. He recognized that the job market for these children was nonexistent. Giving them the opportunity to escape into any kind of beauty could enhance their spirit and give them hope.

Beauty can inspire us. And it becomes our challenge to create it or find it. For some of us, it may simply involve our own way of interacting with the world. For others, it might be painting, music, or literature. But it is there for each of us to seek, to share, and to create.

Self-Mastery as it Relates to a Purpose Statement

PURPOSE: To be a model of possibility for what can be achieved in mid-life and beyond, to attain self-mastery, and to make every room I enter a better room.

My purpose statement refers to three things. First, being a model of possibility means showing those who believe that "it can't be done" that perhaps it can. That means proving it to myself as well. Whether it's being paid to play music for large crowds, write books, or maintain an excellent physique with an equivalent level of health and fitness, I am striving to reach the upper limits of my genetic potential at all times. Hopefully, it will inspire others who are interested to see that you can attain stretch goals at any age – while still just being regular folks.

The second clause in my purpose statement talks about attaining self-mastery. Self-mastery is a highly individualized pursuit. What I conceive of as self-mastery for me, would probably be ill-conceived for anyone else. In fact, I would suspect that my thoughts on self-mastery might be a bit "far out" for most. Much of it relates to the kind of impulse control that we learned about earlier.

Beyond simply enhancing impulse control and being able to delay gratification, moving towards my own self-mastery means learning to live without approval, appreciation and affection. Don't get me wrong, those are wonderful things to receive and many would argue that they are essential to life. And I am not suggesting that you turn away from them when offered. But I believe that the key is in not *needing* those things in order to flourish and be happy. Because for many in our culture, approval, appreciation and affection go away as we age. Age is not revered in traditional Western societies. In fact, it is shunned, feared and avoided at all costs.

When we learn to live without the need for approval, appreciation and affection, we become completely self-contained. No one has leverage on us. *We begin to approach mastery.*

In our culture, the need for approval has reached a neurotic epidemic. We only have to look at our preoccupation with such social media as Facebook. People get an addictive dopamine hit when someone "likes" them on Facebook. For some, it becomes a never-ending quest to obtain approval. Getting approval from others is a wonderful thing; but we must be careful that it doesn't become a neurotic need. We are all susceptible to this so please don't read into this that I'm above it. I've experienced it first-hand. Having a healthy ego, I know the slippery slope to where this path can lead.

It's important to note that there can be a huge upside to Facebook and other social media. We can catch up with old friends and stay in touch with family. Perhaps people can even form deeper connections. But I believe those deeper connections are the exception rather than the rule. I've seen people design perfect "avatar-like" social media existences that have no relation to their own actual reality. This typically ends up creating a profound loneliness because no real connection exists.

It can also lead to unbelievable absurdities. If you think I'm exaggerating, just recall former Notre Dame linebacker Manti Te'o, currently a San Diego Charger. He was the football player who had a relationship with an on-line girlfriend that wasn't real. And once he realized she wasn't real, he kept up the façade that she was.

This is not normal.

Of course, I believe that we never have to be lonely if we enjoy our own company. By becoming more interesting people, we won't need to have other people entertaining us all the time. We can easily enjoy our alone time if we have cultivated a number of interests.

In chapter two, we talked about fighting societal programming. This requires that we remain independent of the good opinion of others. It obliges us to call upon a certain strength and willingness to remain steadfast in solitude. It necessitates becoming an adult.

What does it mean to be an adult? It has nothing to do with age. We may be sixty years old and still not be an adult. It has everything to do with maturity and wisdom. Many people never attain either. Here are thirteen attributes that I believe define actual adult behaviors.

ADULTS...

- Soothe their own bad feelings
- Pursue their own goals
- Stand on their own two feet
- Are self differentiated and place responsibility where it belongs

- Are non-anxious
- Are present with those they are leading
- Separate from surrounding emotional processes
- Persist in facing resistance
- Self-regulate emotions in the presence of sabotage
- Are willing to take a stand and risk displeasing others
- Recognize that it isn't always easy and it isn't always fair
- Lead by example and understand that everybody is watching them
- Make their capabilities exceed their limitations

I realize that by this definition, a very small percentage of the population is actually adult. But we can see where learning to live without approval, appreciation and affection fits within these attributes.

For some, the term "becoming an adult" or using the phrase "grow up" are used in a manipulative fashion. People will use them to try and get you to conform to whatever social convention they want you to embrace. In fact, I believe that becoming an adult and growing up simply come down to accepting responsibility for your behavior. It has nothing to do with buying in to society's norms. In my world, accepting the consequences that come with whatever you're doing means you're on your way to adulthood.

Not Being Appreciated? What Are You Not Giving?

In accordance with giving up the need for being appreciated, you may find that the accolades you used to routinely receive begin slipping away as you age. If you choose to move out of business and competitive pursuits, it's almost inevitable. Don't despair. This is normal and not to be feared. Just like everything else is to a master, it is to be used.

So just how are we to use this? What are we to do?

I believe that typically, the very things that we believe are missing in our lives are exactly what we need to be giving. If we place our focus on "giving" approval, appreciation and affection where and when appropriate, we can guarantee that the rest of our lives will be of value in service to others. Not being attached to what we get in return is where the master lives. It is imperative that we get beyond the need to have things go our way. Attaining mastery means that we get past that with the understanding that fairness is not a concept rooted in reality.

Let's examine fairness for a moment. As Dennis Wholey once said, "Expecting the world to treat you fairly because you are good is like expecting the bull not to charge because you are a vegetarian." Life just doesn't work that way.

As children, we often get programmed to believe that life is supposed to be fair. Our well-meaning parents don't want to give preferential treatment to any of their offspring. As a result, they attempt to keep the score even. If one child gets two pieces of cake, the other gets two pieces as well. This leads to an entitlement mentality. We begin to believe that we should all get what everyone else gets. When that doesn't happen, we get frustrated. Then, once we understand that things are not fair, we ultimately recognize that nature is elitist. And by definition, not everyone can be a member of an elite group.

Nature has established an aristocracy of merit. Those who are most fit to survive, intellectually, physically, or both – tend to do well in a world that is characterized by competition. And competition exists. We can ignore it, but it exists independently of our opinion about it.

Humans crave wealth, status, beauty, intelligence and power. We just do. And we compete for them accordingly.

I remember when a California government committee in the 1980's was commissioned to study self-esteem. The belief was that every child should feel worthy. This led to the idea that every child should get a participation trophy so that they would feel good about themselves. The thought was that feeling good about one's self would lead to self-esteem. And a person with self-esteem would more likely be an achiever and a productive member of society. Nice idea but it turned out that self-esteem and productivity are not necessarily causal or even correlated.

Within the last thirty years, we have found that feeling good about yourself is just as likely to make you feel entitled as it is to be productive. This feeling of entitlement is a direct result of a skewed belief that life should be fair and that everyone should be a winner.

Of course, in direct opposition to this, many of us believe that the people who provide value should be the winners and reap the rewards of their effort. Perhaps if those who are not providing value felt less good about themselves, they might suck it up and generate more worth. They might learn to embrace the discomfort that almost always comes with achievement and the production of value.

Discomfort is also important to address within the concept of mastery. Growth only comes when we are forced to feel uncomfortable. What makes us uncomfortable may vary from person to person. For some, public speaking may make them uncomfortable. For others it might be hard physical exercise. Whatever it is, only by leaning into the discomfort of a stretch goal and taking action can we grow towards the upper limits of our genetic potential.

Masters continually place themselves in uncomfortable situations. Ultimately, they become comfortable within the discomfort. The ordinary among us are only concerned with remaining comfortable. The problem becomes when we begin to depend so much on the things that make us comfortable that we believe we can't live without them. It's a problem when what was once only convenient becomes a necessity.

Convenience vs. Necessity

Growing up in Chicago, I got my first and only bicycle when I was six years old. I had it for one day before it was stolen. The bike would have made my life more convenient. But I didn't have one so I walked. A lot. It's a big town. By most accounts, I turned out okay, though I never learned to ride a bike, which today, way too many people find humorous.

I used to boil water for instant coffee. (What? Yes, I drink instant coffee.) Now I use the microwave. It's more convenient, but I wouldn't die if I had to boil water. And many of you are probably saying, "I'd die before I'd drink instant coffee." That's exactly my point.

Before Global Positioning Systems (GPS) I would look up driving directions on the Internet. Before the Internet, I went to the gas station and bought a map. The GPS is more convenient, but I don't *have* to have it. I always got where I was going just fine.

I don't need an "app" on my iPhone to tell me what I'm supposed to do. It's convenient, but I don't *need* it. I'm an adult. I'll figure it out.

The point here is simply that necessity is relative. Masters figure out ways to solve problems even when the technology goes down. And I love technology; that's not the message here. Without technology, specifically, cataract surgery, I'd be blind in one eye. So I'm a fan. The message is to simply stay conscious of what you believe is essential as opposed to what isn't.

The third clause in my purpose statement points back to the Cassandra story I shared in Chapter three. Making every room I enter a better room sounds pretty corny on the surface. And I fail at it every day. But if I keep that idea in front of me and hold it in my awareness, my relationships improve. In addition, my contributions and service to the world are almost guaranteed simply by holding this thought. It is the very element that could turn the tide in making the last thing I ever do, the greatest thing I ever do.

Age as a Competitive Advantage

People just seem to assume that younger is better. Certainly, if you're running a 100 meter race, it probably is. But many of the things that come with youth do not help when pitted against the baby boomers. Yet we in the senior sector also seem to buy in to the notion that younger people have more competitive advantages. (Again, we're being conditioned and programmed to believe something that is not necessarily rooted in reality.)

True, younger folks probably have an edge in their comfort with technology. But there's nothing about a computer or an iPhone that can't be learned. On the flip side, you can't teach experience. You have to actually go through life to get the knowledge and wisdom that come with experience.

Here are how I see some advantages and disadvantages of "Younger vs. Older." (I'm speaking in generalities so there will always be exceptions.)

Generally speaking, the older crowd:

1. Is more well-read and literate.
2. Is not addicted to their phone.
3. Is more patient.
4. Is physically and mentally tougher, much tougher.
5. Is more easily able to resolve conflict.
6. Have more references from which to make better decisions.
7. Is less distracted.
8. Is able to focus more on the task at hand.
9. Is able to stay with a problem longer before giving up.
10. Is less likely to be caught up in idle chatter.

11. Is less likely to be texting while driving.
12. Is more in tune with current events that have nothing to do with the Kardashians or Game of Thrones.
13. Is more likely to know the names of the president and vice-president (seriously).

I could go on, but you get the idea. There's a lot to like about being older. And frankly, if you've stayed in great physical condition, you can have the best of both worlds. You can have the body of a kid and the wisdom of middle age and beyond. That's a formidable combination.

If you haven't stayed in great physical shape, you can still improve from where you're at. It's just a little more difficult but definitely worth the effort.

Mastery Involves Flourishing Under Stress and Pressure

Masters never run from pressure. In fact, masters run toward it, lean into it and flourish within it. Typically, they are more apt to respond to pressure and then put the pressure on others. (I don't *have* stress; I *give* stress.)

Stress is viewed as positive by a master. It is fuel to move us forward. And mostly, stress is mental pressure we put on ourselves. Or we allow someone else to rent space in our head and we feel their push.

Typically, we don't rise to the stress of a situation as much as we fall to the level of our training and preparation. As such, readying ourselves for stress and pressure can mean the difference between success and failure.

Mastery Has No Room for Jealousy

Masters recognize that they cannot legislate how others feel or what they do. They cannot legislate what others value. Nor can they control what others accomplish. All they can do is hold themselves and others accountable for whatever responsibilities they've agreed upon.

If you are in a love relationship, why would you want to hold your beloved hostage and demand that they feel and behave a certain way? Yet that's our traditional default position. It's positively ludicrous, yet we've all done it.

Allowing the people that you supposedly love to exercise their preferences seems like a more loving response to me. And who wouldn't want to be around someone like that?

That doesn't mean that we should ever put up with abuse. Nor do we need to allow others to take advantage of us. But it's useful to recognize that people are going to feel what they feel and do what they do. Let them. Relax. Chill. You will only breed resentment and hostility if you try and force others into a box.

Once we've approached mastery, we become secure in our own worth. What others do becomes secondary. At that point, we can be happy to see others fulfill themselves in whatever way they choose. And we know how to take care of ourselves.

Furthermore, if others are successful, rather than be jealous of them, learn from them. You can remain a strong competitive force without being jealous. Congratulate others on their success and examine what you might emulate in order to make yourself more successful. Like its siblings, cynicism and bitterness, jealousy is a useless emotion.

Mastery Also Involves Addressing the Seven Fears

I have identified seven "core" fears that I believe most humans face during their lifetime. They are:

1. Fear of pain
2. Fear of death
3. Fear of not living fully
4. Fear of disapproval (humiliation, shame, etc.)
5. Fear of poverty/lack
6. Fear of loss
7. Fear of isolation

As mentioned in the segment on offensive mindset, fear is essentially a conversation we have with ourselves about what we think we know. It typically involves what we think is going to happen in the future.

With the exception of pain, which is real, everything else on this list is mental. Our fears live only in our mind. And even pain becomes worse when we let our mind run away with it. To achieve mastery, each of us must figure out our own strategies to deal with fear, because we will all face each of these at some point.

Let's look at each of these fears in order.

Fear number one is pain. Pain is mandatory, we'll all have some. Suffering, however, is optional. Suffering involves telling ourselves how awful the pain is and how we'll never be able to live with it into the future. If we continue along that thinking path, we'll soon be candidates for the crazy train. But the fact is, we may be living with it now – and as bad as it is, we seem able to stand it.

Chronic pain is difficult. Experts in treating chronic pain sometimes advocate staying present with it. Turning the pain over in the mind and looking at how it is handled moment to moment has helped many people retain their sanity while living in pain.

I advocate pain management clinics for those in chronic pain – and I have tremendous respect for those who manage it and continue forward.

Fear number two is death. We'll certainly die eventually. As such, we may believe that we haven't done enough to live fully in our life. That's fear number three. Having your own bucket list can help with this. Figuring out what is still left to do and executing on that list will help you handle both fears two and three. But you must take action. And when you act, you risk facing fear number four, disapproval.

Fear of disapproval is perhaps the number one neurosis in our culture. While we don't necessarily seek disapproval, it's going to come to each of us at some point. But masters often embrace disapproval, recognizing its inevitability and the opportunity to grow in the face of it. They shrug off embarrassment as part of being engaged in life. If you go after a "big" life, people are going to disapprove. Masters ignore these critics, preferring to risk failure and disapproval, rather than always playing it safe.

Fear number five is lack. Masters do not worry about lack. They don't believe in it. They are so confident that even if they get wiped out financially, they know they'll be back. They are typically very generous because they know that if they run low, in an abundant universe, they'll always figure out a way to get more.

Fear number six is loss. Like death, we will all experience loss. We lose friends, spouses, parents, siblings and all kinds of material possessions. Fearing these things is normal but masters do not waste emotion on it. They are grateful for what they've had – and they move on. They recognize that the sooner they get on with life, the less time they have lost.

The last fear is isolation. Masters do not fear isolation because they love their own company. They have already faced their mental demons and are not afraid to be alone with their own minds. Those who must always be busy or entertained, and cannot sit quietly in a room alone, will never achieve mastery. They have not yet mastered and tamed their own minds.

Portrait of a Person Who Has Achieved Mastery: The Next Stage in Evolution

Once we begin to approach what I call "mental toughness mastery," we can begin to choose personal fulfillment in circumstances where others fall apart. We don't always succeed. But it's directional. Can we approach this ideal more often than not? Can we flourish without the approval of those around us? Can we contribute silently and even anonymously knowing that no appreciation is forthcoming? Can we press forward when no one is affectionate towards us?

Perhaps Rudyard Kipling said it best over 100 years ago.

IF
‾‾

IF you can keep your head when all about you
Are losing theirs and blaming it on you,
If you can trust yourself when all men doubt you,
But make allowance for their doubting too;
If you can wait and not be tired by waiting,

Or being lied about, don't deal in lies,
Or being hated, don't give way to hating,
And yet don't look too good, nor talk too wise:

If you can dream - and not make dreams your master;
If you can think - and not make thoughts your aim;
If you can meet with Triumph and Disaster
And treat those two impostors just the same;
If you can bear to hear the truth you've spoken
Twisted by knaves to make a trap for fools,
Or watch the things you gave your life to, broken,
And stoop and build 'em up with worn-out tools:

If you can make one heap of all your winnings
And risk it on one turn of pitch-and-toss,
And lose, and start again at your beginnings
And never breathe a word about your loss;
If you can force your heart and nerve and sinew
To serve your turn long after they are gone,
And so hold on when there is nothing in you
Except the Will which says to them: 'Hold on!'

If you can talk with crowds and keep your virtue,
' Or walk with Kings - nor lose the common touch,
if neither foes nor loving friends can hurt you,
If all men count with you, but none too much;
If you can fill the unforgiving minute
With sixty seconds' worth of distance run,
Yours is the Earth and everything that's in it,
And - which is more - you'll be a Man, my son!

Rudyard Kipling understood mastery.

The Code of Mental Toughness

It is one thing to study mental toughness but entirely another to practice it. To attain mastery, we must practice. Proper practice requires intention and mindful awareness of what we are practicing. I developed the code below to remind myself of specific actions that I must do or not do to attain mastery. (The words in italics provide a shortened version of the code.)

Swagger at 60: The Code of Mental Toughness

1. *I will show up and "bring it" every day.* (Whether a good day or a bad day, I will show up with presence and intention.)
2. *I will not complain nor make excuses.* (Complaining is the refuge of those who have no self-reliance.)
3. *I will remain effective without needing approval, appreciation and affection,* although I enjoy them. (The best life is lived in self-mastery with an ability to soothe one's self in difficult times.)
4. *I will remain a non-anxious presence in the midst of turmoil* by separating myself from surrounding emotional processes.
5. *I will differentiate myself from others* and place responsibility for actions and feelings where they belong.

6. *I will lead by example*, understanding that it isn't always easy and it isn't always fair.
7. *I will relentlessly focus on solutions* and not fixate on the problems.

SECTION III:

WHAT I'VE LEARNED

CHAPTER SIX – *The Swagger at 60 Prescriptions*

Being 60 comes with many opinions. One trusts that it also comes with some wisdom. Chapter six documents what I hope will serve as some prescriptive wisdom garnered from success, failure, several wins and many losses. Rather than learn from my own mistakes, I've always preferred to learn from some other poor bastard's – but I've still made my share.

Hopefully, a few of these prescriptions will get you to consider some alternative ways of being. If you can learn from my failures, I can be your version of some other poor bastard. Some of these gems are a little provocative, caustic and perhaps sarcastic. They may annoy and/or irritate you. I'm okay with that.

Enjoy.

LIFE IS A GAME – MIGHT AS WELL PLAY TO WIN

Life is like a board game and the object is to win. But what is winning? You have to define what winning looks like for you. For many, it means doing more of what you want to do, and less of what you don't.

For me, winning involves learning how to make myself happy under any circumstance. And happiness for me involves some level of self-development and achievement. It means acquisition of pleasure (both short and long-term) and minimization of pain, recognizing that occasionally the pain of self-discipline results in a greater long term pleasure. For me, winning requires fulfilling or making manifest my own human nature –satisfying my inner drives. In addition to my basic drives for air, food, water, shelter, and connection, this will generally mean that I will continue to grow in the areas that interest me. Winning is also having good health and in the absence of that, making my capabilities exceed my limitations – being the best with what I have.

FIGURE OUT THE MINIMUM EFFECTIVE DOSE

It only takes one well-placed shot to kill a deer. More than that and you begin to destroy the meat – to say nothing of wasting time and effort. Do what you need to do quickly and efficiently. Then move on to the next kill.

STOP GOLD-PLATING EVERYTHING AND RELEASE THE PRODUCT

We are all raised to "do our best." Generally, that's great advice. But sometimes the perfect is the enemy of the good. Our desire to be perfect can get in the way of our actually *doing anything*! If you're waiting for something to be perfect before releasing it, it's likely that you will never produce anything. Sometimes we need to launch while Beta-testing and then iterate the product until it's perfect. Otherwise, we become paralyzed.

"FAST AND ADEQUATE" VERSUS "SLOW AND BETTER"

Sometimes it is simply about doing an adequate job in an inadequate amount of time. There are times when you just cannot be late with a product. At those times, "fit for use" is often good enough.

THE MOST IMPORTANT MEAL OF THE DAY IS THE ONE YOU DON'T EAT

Generally speaking, in the United States, we eat too much. Our statistics on obesity are chilling. Our abundance is killing us. We have food channels, for God's sakes. Even Ben Franklin said, "To lengthen thy life, lessen thy meals." Not only will it not kill you to miss a meal, it will probably do you a lot of good.

ADHERE TO MY FIVE WORD INFORMERCIAL

Eat less. Eat better. Exercise.

STOP GIVING YOUR POWER AWAY

Sticks and stones, people. You can't offend me. I won't give you that. If you call me a name and I'm offended, I've given you control over me. Why on earth would I do that? I'm not a victim. You're the idiot calling me a name. Hey, wait, I just called you an idiot. Are you offended? (I love the power I have over you.)

TWO OF THE MOST IMPORTANT WORDS YOU'LL EVER USE

No, the words are not "please" and "thank you," although they are important. The words are "choice" and "inconvenient." I know, not very sexy. But our lives are directed by choice. The road we choose determines everything. And when we choose badly, instead of making it a tragedy and the end of the world, make it…inconvenient. Using that word to describe something that is seemingly awful, can actually make it humorous – or at least, palatable.

THE MOST DANGEROUS PERSON IS THE ONE WHO PERCEIVES HE HAS NOTHING TO LOSE

The person who believes he has nothing to lose is not risk averse. There is no risk because nothing, not even his life, means anything. This is a very powerful position and one worth considering occasionally, even if it is irrational. It's amazing what you can get done when your back is against the wall and there's nothing to lose. Think about it. People will get out of your way if they believe you don't care about consequences.

TO FIND OUT WHY – FOLLOW THE MONEY OR THE SEX

We may find ourselves occasionally wondering why a particular decision was made. In most cases, if you follow the money trail, you'll get an answer. The other great motivator is sex. Humans will go to a lot of trouble and take great risks to satisfy this natural, but often frowned-upon urge. (It's typically most frowned upon by the people not having it.) At the risk of violating the sensibilities of the innocent and tender-minded, it almost always comes down to "who is getting paid and who is getting laid."

KEEP AN OPEN MIND

We don't know everything. And we certainly don't know what we don't know. Getting set in our ways can keep us from growth. For example, during my entire powerlifting and bodybuilding career, I've always maintained that eating four to six small meals per day was the best way to go. That was the common wisdom. And while at some level, doing that worked for me, I recently tried something else. Wanting to drop some body fat while keeping muscle, I became intrigued with the research around intermittent fasting (I.F.). After looking at some of the science as well as anecdotal evidence, I began to experiment with some of the I.F.

concepts. After a six month period, I went from 157 pounds to 142 and saw an amazing drop in body fat. I became vascular, striated and perhaps even more significantly, my biomarkers of health improved. The lesson for me was that it's worthwhile to occasionally entertain some new ideas.

IF WE ALWAYS DO WHAT WE'VE ALWAYS DONE...

In conjunction with keeping an open mind, it's useful to consider that if we always do what we've always done, we'll get what we've always got. If I eat and exercise in the same fashion for years on end, I can't expect for much significant change to occur. If I continue to treat people badly...well, you get the idea.

DIFFERENTIATE YOURSELF

Figure out what is unique about you and exploit that in the service of others. Even if it's just that you'll work harder and do the jobs no one else will, that's still a differentiator. Think of that TV show, Dirty Jobs, on the Discovery Channel. If you're willing to do it, there's a job for you. What are you bringing to the table that no one else can – or will?

DON'T BE YOURSELF – BE YOUR *BEST* SELF

Once you know what is unique about you, bring your best attention, intention and energy to as many present moments as possible. This will become your authentic *best* self. Of course, it's fine to let down occasionally. I sometimes need to be that schlub on the couch watching the game. But for too many folks, that's their authentic best self. Unless you've chosen to give up, don't let that happen to you.

SELF-AWARENESS OF A WEAKNESS IS NOT THE SAME AS SELF-DOUBT

Knowing that you are not strong in a particular area can allow you to shore it up if it's a problem. If it's not a problem, ignore it. I'm horrible at car repair. But I have no interest in learning the fundamentals of car maintenance. As a result, I pay someone to do it. In fact, I went to college so I wouldn't have to do it…and I don't.

REINTRODUCE CHARM

Charm has practically disappeared in our culture. It's so easy to find what is wrong with everyone. It's like shooting fish in a barrel. We can find seven things wrong with someone before we even blink. Then we tell them in the interest of giving them helpful "feedback." I think it is much more interesting to home in on what is terrific about someone – and then to share that. People so rarely hear the good about themselves. And if you show enthusiasm for their successes, you'll have a friend and ally for life.

ASKING SOMEONE FOR ADVICE IS A GREAT COMPLIMENT

People love being asked for advice. It shows that you respect their opinion and makes them feel valued. And hey, you might just get some great guidance.

CONFLICT AVOIDANCE

Conflict is often positive and necessary in order to come up with solutions. However, too often it's drummed up simply because we want someone else to be different than they are – which leads to the next point…

ARGUING IS A WASTE OF TIME

There is no point in arguing with people who have already made up their minds. Getting them to be different or to change their opinion is an unbelievable long shot. We waste time and energy and everyone ends up frustrated or angry. If we simply need to be on the record, fine. Beyond that, let it go.

DO NOT SPEAK IN ORDER TO RELIEVE YOUR STRESS

It will feel good in the moment. You'll feel smart. You'll feel victorious. You'll be right. You'll have won! But once the alimony and child support payments begin, you'll wish you had used a glue stick instead of

Chap Stick. Sometimes it's just better to walk away and "do not speak."

SOME THINGS ARE MORE IMPORTANT THAN YOUR FEAR

Whether a great cause, a worthwhile risk, or simply saving a life; some things are more important than your fear. Consider that; then do what needs doing.

ACT IN THE FACE OF YOUR FEAR

I am neurotically compelled to do things I'm afraid of. I'm afraid of heights so, in my early twenties, no doubt before my neocortex was completely developed, I jumped off the fourth floor balcony of the Daytona Beach Days Inn. Fortunately, I landed in their swimming pool. But wait, there's more. I then skydived. In my thirties I began bungee jumping. Why? Because I was scared. But the fear of not doing these things was greater than my actual fear of doing them. I just always believed that if I was scared to do something, it meant that I should probably do it. (But notice I used the words "neurotically compelled." Things like drugs, thugs and poisonous bugs are best left alone. No need to take everything on just because it is scary. Now that I'm a little older, I get that.)

LIVE AND LET LIVE – PART ONE

After being on the planet for 60 years, here's my conclusion. As an adult, the right to flail your arms and fist ends at the bridge of my nose. Beyond that, if you're paying your own way, you should do whatever you want. For me to try and control your behavior and what you want is just silly. I am not taking hostages. Go where you want to. Sleep with whomever you want to. Party as long as you want to. Of course, you still have to accept the consequences for whatever you're doing. And you need to pay your own way. If you're not paying, then you'll need to answer to whoever is because in essence, he or she is your employer. Having said that; go get 'em!

LIVE AND LET LIVE – PART TWO

I don't care if you're Catholic, Protestant, Muslim, Hindu, Mormon, Buddhist, or worshipping goats. Have at it. (I believe that at last count we had three "one true" Gods.) But please try and stop killing anyone that doesn't believe what you believe. Yes, I know; you're right and they're wrong. So how 'bout we just let them be wrong. It won't hurt, I promise. (Plus, it's easier for me to read without the bombings, beheadings and commotion.)

BE MINDFUL OF YOUR DEPENDENCIES

In a recent study, 88 percent of people between the ages of 18 and 24 said that their mobile phone was more important than the Internet, deodorant and their toothbrush. No further commentary necessary.

UNDERSTAND THAT YOU WILL NOT BE "UNDERSTOOD"

Practically no one is going to "get" you. Once you realize you don't have to be understood, you can relax. Stop explaining yourself to everyone. If you're paying your own way and harming no one else, you don't need to justify anything to anybody. Trying to get people to understand you is just more time lost.

BE CAREFUL OF WHAT DEFINES YOU

Instead of being peer-dependent, status-conscious, narcissistic consumers, we can choose to enjoy material possessions without being defined by them. It's great to arrive at my problems in the Lexus, but it's perfectly okay to arrive at them in the Yaris. I'm competent to solve the problem in either case.

WHO YOU TRULY ARE SHOWS UP UNDER STRESS AND PRESSURE

When the chips are down and the game is on the line, do you panic? Do you start blaming others and running from the problem? Or do you stay calm, step up and work towards a solution. Whichever of those two options you choose, that's who you are.

LEADERS ARE MAKERS OF MOOD

If you are a true leader, the environment will reflect your leadership. Your team will reflect your personality. You can set a tone of fear or a tone of productive and fun challenge. To lead means to go first. Be the first to sacrifice. If you sacrifice for your team, they will sacrifice for you. Be the first to trust. Be the first to risk. They will follow your lead. If not, get a new team.

GREAT LEADERS NEVER SACRIFICE PEOPLE TO MAKE THE NUMBERS

Some will disagree with me on this one. But the vast majority of leaders only think of next quarter's profits. Thus, they will lay people off to make their numbers. Outstanding leaders never sacrifice people to make the numbers. They will find a way to get the money in some other fashion. They will put themselves in harm's way to protect their employees. Investors won't like that. But the employees will – and they will carry that leader to victory down the road. This requires patience; an almost unknown commodity in today's business environment.

BE CAREFUL NOT TO MISTAKE SINCERITY FOR TRUTH

Some people are often wrong but never uncertain. Always check the facts.

JUST BECAUSE SOMETHING IS POLITICALLY INCORRECT DOES NOT MAKE IT FALSE

If someone says something that makes you wince, that doesn't automatically mean it's untrue. Don't let unpleasant or blunt words spoken by a boorish person allow you to believe that they may not be accurate. Sometimes even cretins speak the truth. Again, check the facts.

YOU ARE GOING TO JUDGE OTHERS, SO DO IT WELL

What are they saying? Do I agree? Are they saying anything remotely intelligent? What does their physical presence say about them? These are the unconscious questions we ask ourselves when we initially judge someone. It might be more useful to temporarily suspend judgment until we can observe their behaviors. I tend to positively evaluate people who get things done in an effective and efficient manner. I tend to negatively evaluate people who are very busy but unproductive. There is typically a lot of talk, drama, commotion and emotion that go along with that. Busy is busy.

Productive is productive. There's a difference. To the extent possible, associate with the productive people.

HANG WITH A BETTER CROWD

There is some thought that your income is the average of your six closest friends. As such, I'm always trying to trade up. I want to hang with people who are smarter, wealthier and more accomplished than me. Those who are poor, unhappy, and out of shape will be more than happy to drag me down with them. They often see themselves as victims. If you are spending time in the victim support chat room, that's who you are. To the extent possible, move onward and upward. You get what you focus on. Don't fall in love with being a victim. Seek out winners and be one.

THERE IS NOTHING SPIRITUAL ABOUT POVERTY

You cannot help the world if you don't have resources. Many people still believe that money is the root of all evil. No. Being a drain on society and the tax base is evil. Creating value and receiving wealth is goodness. You can't help anyone if you have nothing. I recommend making a boatload of money and then building an orphanage. That's how it's done.

CALLER I.D. IS GOD

It is rare when anyone calls me offering something for nothing. In fact, it's happened once in the last five years. One of the gals in my band called and offered to bring me a Starbucks, no questions asked. It was thrilling. Typically, my home phone makes me wonder if the voice mail message says, "I'm your personal favor-grantor and I have unlimited wealth. Call me anytime with any request because I have no boundaries and I am only here to be used and to give all of my money and time to you. It's what I live for. Please leave a message."

FIGURE OUT WHAT BUSINESS YOU'RE REALLY IN

When I'm done with my day job, I run a successful cover band. We play music. But we're not in the music business. We're in the entertainment business. Even more – we're in the customer service business. We're in whatever business the people that pay us want us to be in for that show. As such, we play terrific venues like Key Arena, the Columbia Tower, and exclusive hotels for an often wealthy and elite clientele. If we were all about our egos and not all about the customer, we'd be playing in my garage.

AND ONCE YOU KNOW WHAT BUSINESS YOU'RE REALLY IN...

Our musical enterprise, The BrickHouse Band, refuses to compete on price. We compete on value. We solve your problems and relieve your pain. Whether it's a corporate party you're throwing or a high-end wedding reception, we will remove your stress. Of course, this actually requires communicating with the customer in order to understand their stress. So have no fear. We've arrived; you can stop worrying now. We're worth what you're paying. *But you probably can't afford us.*

PUT YOUR OWN OXYGEN MASK ON FIRST

It's difficult to help anyone else if you are not stable. I take care of myself first. I schedule self-care. And if I'm scheduled to work out, meditate or study, only an emergency with the spillage of blood is going to pull me away. Why? Because you're not going to pay for my health care. And you're not going to save me. Nor should you. I am responsible for my own well-being. When I'm solid and good to go, then I am better prepared to assist you. And if you're not on board for me taking of myself, you are not in my best interests and it would be best if you would just leave, now.

SET BOUNDARIES

Having set a boundary, there may be a tendency to feel guilty because you're putting your own oxygen mask on before doing anyone else's bidding. Get over it. Unless your insurance policy is over the moon, you can't help them from the coffin.

IT'S TYPICALLY NOT ABOUT YOU

Because we are the centers of our own universe, we tend to overemphasize our own importance. People are generally not thinking much about me when they make decisions. (I know, hard to imagine.) It also rarely pays to attribute motives to other people. If we think that we know why they're doing something and we're wrong, our minds can take us off in a direction that is completely out of line with reality. This can ruin relationships and make us miserable. Remember, it's probably not about you.

IF YOU ARE IN A FAIR FIGHT, YOU DIDN'T PLAN PROPERLY

Have you ever heard the old saying, "All is fair in love and war?" I won't speak to love but you better believe that anything goes in war. War is about winning because loss means death or devastating debilitation. Fair fights are for chumps. Winning fights is for champs. If you haven't been the one to set the context in the fight that you're in, you didn't prepare properly. Win – even if that means taking your chances at trial. At least you'll be alive to face the jury.

HAVE A TOLERANCE FOR STUPIDITY AND JUST GO AROUND IT

Sometimes you have to pay the "stupid tax." Look, there will always be bureaucracy. There will always be signs saying "Do Not Enter" and "No Parking" that no longer apply but are enforced anyway. There will always be rules that serve no purpose. There will always be an empty HOV lane while you and 3,000 other people haven't moved an inch in ten minutes. So occasionally, you just need to shrug it off and exercise patience. Other times, you'll need to break the rules. But if you break them or circumvent them, do it quietly and without fanfare. You don't need to brag. You just need to win.

DO EVERYTHING WITH A PURPOSE

If I'm reading, I'm doing it to learn something or perhaps be entertained. If I'm exercising, I'm doing it to become bigger, stronger, faster, and tougher. If I'm writing, I'm doing it to instruct or amuse readers. If I'm playing music, I'm attempting to entertain or actualize my talent. But there is always a purpose. Overall, my purpose is to better myself; physically, mentally, artistically and financially. Whatever is not those things is a waste of time. (So if you're talking to me about nothing, please stop.)

STOP OVERFUNCTIONING AND "FIXING" PEOPLE

We don't need to rescue everyone. We don't need to tell everyone else how they should be living – even though I'm sort of doing that now. (I love irony.) We don't need to correct everyone's grammar and punctuation. We don't need to convert everyone to our religion. We don't need to tell them what stock to buy or how to fold their laundry. We don't need to bang the drum and make a ruckus for causes that no one cares about. We don't need to stick our noses into everyone else's business. And we certainly don't need to try to enforce rules that have nothing to do with us. Puhleeeeze...STOP!

STOP ROACH STOMPING

And while we're at it, let's stop roach stomping. Little things take up time and wear us out. They keep us from focusing on what matters. We don't need to pay attention to every gnat buzzing about. Focus on the important. For example, if it doesn't concern you, let other people make their own mistakes (see item directly above). They'll learn or they won't. Trust me, most don't want your feedback, even if they act like they do. And you're wasting precious time.

SOME PEOPLE ARE SUPPOSED TO BE HOMELESS AND BROKE

You can give some folks a job and $100, 000 dollars and within six months they'll be back on the street. It's where they're supposed to be in this particular life's evolution. They are just not going to learn the lesson. And now that you've given them $100,000, hopefully, you've learned yours.

YOUR GREATEST GIFT: FIRST, DO NO HARM

Do you really want to make a contribution to society? You can begin by not being a burden to it. Start by working more on yourself and less on everyone else. Get an education. Get healthy. Get a job and create value. Become self-supporting. Pay your student loans. Put some money away. Contribute to the tax base. Once you can support yourself, then consider having children whom you can also support. Imagine how many problems would disappear if everyone simply handled their own stuff. What a gift to the world.

USE THAT CHIP ON YOUR SHOULDER

Unless you were born with tendencies towards narcissism or a psychopathic personality, you probably felt inferior growing up. If we think of the average teenager, we can see the awkwardness, or even the bravado designed to hide the self-consciousness that those trying to fit in display. What human being hasn't experienced rejection, loss or even some form of abuse along the way? Probably not too many. Put a chip on your shoulder and use it to give you an edge. Show anyone who ever slighted you what true greatness is. The best revenge is always a great life.

WE NEED NOT BE SHEEP

At the risk of sounding harsh, the vast majority of people are sheep. They are scared. They are full of self-doubt. Most are consumer-driven and short term thinkers. They want someone to lead them and tell them what to do. If you don't believe this, walk into any conference room or restaurant in America. In a loud and commanding voice, say, "Excuse me everyone. I need you to come with me now!" Then start walking. About 70 percent will get up and follow you. The other 30 percent need more convincing. Be one of the 30 percent.

CHOOSE TO SEE THE PAST AS AN EDUCATION RATHER THAN A BURDEN

The past can either educate us or be something we carry as failure. Most of us don't drive our cars with our eyes focused on the rearview mirror. Yet sometimes we do that with our lives. Look out at what's in front of you. Check the rearview occasionally. And avoid the same kind of accident twice.

SUSPEND YOUR PRECONCEIVED NOTIONS

We often believe that we're only capable of so much. In reality, we can do much more if we give up our preconceived notions about ourselves. We can work out harder, stay up longer, become healthier, make more money, and do so much more than we've been conditioned to believe. But it might hurt a little. There's always a price.

CHOOSE TO BE GREAT

Who are we not to be great? We can choose it. We can choose it physically. We can choose it mentally. We can choose it spiritually, if that's your thing. But we can choose it, starting now. We *know* what to do! The information is available. Let's use the tools of mental toughness to implement what we already know.

HAVE A DIRECTION

In order to choose greatness, we need a direction. Without a direction and target to hit, we're spinning our wheels. Head north. Whether people choose to jump on board or not should be of no consequence. They can keep up or not; doesn't matter. Continue north, with or without anybody else. Set the example.

BE CAREFUL ABOUT TELLING PEOPLE YOUR PLANS – PART ONE

Speaking of moving forward and having a direction, the first thing most of us do when we have an idea is share it. We say that we're going to write a book, start a band, build a business, move to Europe, or something else. The minute we have shared it, we will be told that the idea is ridiculous and unrealistic. Our family, friends, co-workers and practically everyone will try and tell us why we can't. Ignore them. Better yet, just shut up from the get-go. Don't tell anyone your ideas or dreams. Simply create the plan to do what you intend and execute on it. Once it's done, no one will tell you how silly you are.

BE CAREFUL ABOUT TELLING PEOPLE YOUR PLANS – PART TWO

The second reason to not tell people your plans revolves around this question: Don't you get tired of hearing people tell you all of the things they're going to do? Then they don't do them. I have so much respect for people who actually do what they say they're going to do. Even better, I have so much respect for people who just show up with the product. Powerful people tend to speak less and do more. No blah, blah, blah about their plans. I love that.

LIMIT YOUR TRIVIAL CONVERSATIONS

It's appropriate to listen to others and give them respect – until they begin to abuse your time. If someone is prattling on about their relationship or the latest gossip or other things that have absolutely no value, they are not respecting your time. Often, these are people who swear that they don't waste time. And they are always busy, but rarely productive. Be kind to them but extricate yourself from them as quickly as possible. They are a distraction. They are keeping you from the target.

DON'T MAKE FAMILY AND FRIENDS YOUR TOXIC WASTE DUMP

If you saw yourself in the item directly above, be sure and not be an abuser. It's fine to share things about your day but if you are constantly complaining, stop. If you are constantly complaining about the same thing over and over, move out. You are sucking the life and energy out of every room you're in.

IGNORE THE FOOLISHNESS AND THE NUTJOBS

It's important to remain open minded. But be discerning. For example, many people thought that because the Mayan calendar predicted it, the world would end in 2012. Now if they'd have just called a reliable source like The Psychic Hotline, they could have gotten the real scoop.

RECOGNIZE THAT THERE IS A PRICE FOR EVERYTHING

Anything worth having is worth paying for. Be suspicious of the free lunch. Someone is trying to sell you a time share.

CREATE A PROBLEM, SELL THE SOLUTION

Religions, governments, advertisers, pharmaceutical companies and businesses do this all the time. What kind of crisis can you create that only you have the answer to? Now you are a valuable commodity with a fat investment portfolio.

PAY YOUR OWN DAMN WAY – AND THEN PUT A CROWBAR IN YOUR WALLET

Carry your weight. It's always better to have others depend on your generosity than having to depend on theirs. Owing everybody means carrying a lot of extra baggage. If you become so good at what you do that they can't live without you, you won't owe anyone for long. And pick up the tab for God's sake. Put a crowbar in your wallet and share some of your abundance.

NO ONE IS COMING TO SAVE YOU

It's best to assume that no one is coming to bail you out of your problems. Not the government, not the family, not the activists, and certainly not the bureaucrats. If you get some help, terrific. But it's best to plan to handle it yourself.

WHEN YOU HIT YOUR TARGET, STOP!

Execute on your plan. Hit the target. Then make a new plan to execute on your next target. Don't get greedy. Too many people keep thinking that the stock price will continue to go up. Stop when you've succeeded and take the afternoon off.

BEWARE OF FOLLOWING YOUR BLISS

The author of The Power of Myth, Joseph Campbell, probably meant well when he encouraged people to "follow their bliss." Unfortunately, it set a lot of people off in the wrong direction. Unless your bliss is something people will pay for, you're better off making bliss your hobby. For many of us, bliss is our art. And everyone wants to be paid for their art. Everyone. The Federal Bureau of Labor Statistics informs us that artists have an average annual income of $44,380. However, that number is overblown due to the earnings of a few art world superstars.

A separate survey of 1,200 professional artists found that 49 percent made less than $4,900 in the previous year and only 13 percent made more than $25,000. I've managed to build a terrific cover band that plays all over North America and we are paid well relative to our competition. *But it's still not a living!* And that's okay. People pay for my art and that feels good. But I'd advise keeping other streams of income.

HOWEVER, IF YOU CHOOSE TO FOLLOW YOUR BLISS...

If your bliss is your art and you choose to go for it, that's fine. But you better be good and you better believe in yourself. Then you need to jettison the dog, cat, husband, wife, kids, and get absolutely psychotic in going after it. There should be no other purpose to your life. You should be an absolutely annoying, unreasonable, driven, ruthless, and relentless bullet on its way to the target that only death can stop. And like I said, you better be good or at least able to make other people believe that you are.

IT'S CALLED WORK FOR A REASON

We don't call it "going to play." We call it "going to work." You don't need to like it. You just need to *do it.* You simply need to like the results. The outcome is what matters. Use the tools of mental toughness to do whatever needs doing. Do it to the best of your ability, unless "fit for use" makes more sense. Building your skill base and becoming good at something, even if it's not quite what you pictured, can still be quite satisfying. Do what needs to be done. Get paid. Rinse. Repeat.

THERE IS NO SHAME IN WORKING FOR SOMEONE ELSE

I've succeeded (and failed) in both corporate America and as an entrepreneur. Entrepreneurs often take particular pride in being their own boss. But often, they're beholden to creditors, suppliers and other involved parties. In essence, they have bosses too. So ignore anyone who criticizes you because you work for "the man." As long as you're providing value and service, you're good.

AND ABOUT THAT SALARY

We're typically paid in direct proportion to the amount of frustration and large-scale problems we're willing to take on. If you're one of the folks ranting about the minimum wage, think bigger. Always be working on something big.

THERE ARE ALWAYS MORE THINGS TO DO THAN TIME TO DO THEM

There will always be an endless list of things to do. You must choose among them. A useful rule to remember is to knock down the target that is the nearest to creating pain or crisis. This is otherwise known as "the thing that's about to bite your face." Or as a learned Australian once said, "You've got to kill the crocodile closest to the canoe!"

WORK THE HIGHEST LEVERAGED OPPORTUNITIES

Because there are always more things to do than time to do them, we need to identify the highest leveraged opportunities. These are the activities that give us the greatest return on our effort. This is not a fun exercise but remember, everything we do has a cost in terms of time, energy and space. Eliminate without mercy. Give your assistant the lower leveraged activities. What's that? You don't have an assistant? Well, if you don't have an assistant, you are one.

LOVE THE JOBS THAT LOVE YOU BACK

The most inefficient activities are the ones that we love but that don't love us back. Internet surfing that is not target-directed does not love us back. Video games do not love us back. Idle chatter does not love us back. These and other distractions that don't love us back are the difference between making $20,000 and six or seven figures this year. Which tax bracket do you want to be in?

TWO KINDS OF PEOPLE

There are two kinds of people; those who got it done –
and those with all the reasons why they didn't.

PRACTICE AT LEAST ONE MENTAL TOUGHNESS TOOL PER DAY

Your mental toughness muscles only get stronger with
use. Commit to making yourself uncomfortable at least
once per day. Take the stairs instead of the elevator.
Fast for 24 hours. Get up 30 minutes earlier to perform
some self-improvement activity. Take an ice cold
shower. These small commitments will remind you of
just how much control over yourself you actually have.
Stay strong in your practice.

TAKE CHARGE OF WHAT YOU'RE COMMUNICATING

Think of your initial impressions on people. If you were
a billboard, what would they think of you? You are
always communicating. Are you groomed and dressed
well? Are you in good physical condition? Are you
personable, focused and relaxed? Or are you stressed
and distracted? People will decide what they think of
you within the first five to 15 seconds and then they
will work to justify that opinion in order to remain
consistent. If someone else's first impression is
important to you, take charge of it.

ASK BIG!

People will only value you to the level that you value yourself. Ask for *more* money than your competition. Then deliver. There are many wealthy people who feel better about paying more because it makes them feel secure in that they're getting the best. Those are the kind of clients you want. Be the best. Get paid. You're worth it.

ELEVATE YOUR STATUS IN YOUR MARKET

The higher you go up the income ladder, the more you will be paid for *"who you are"* as opposed to what you do or what you sell. People pay more for "status" than ordinary. My PayLess Champion shoes cost $24. My Nikes cost five times that. Yet the Champions always outlast the Nikes. The lesson? People "perceive" that the Nikes are superior. Provide value but always elevate your status in the eyes of your market. Position yourself as an expert and an authority. Move as far away from the lower-tier generalists as possible. Celebrities get paid for simply showing up to events. Be one.

CUSTOMERS ARE MORE ABOUT RELATIONSHIPS THAN COSTS

If someone has a customer that I want, it's not because of a lower price. It's because they have a better relationship with that customer. If people cared only about price, everyone would drive a used VW, wear

Thrift Shop clothes and listen to the radio. Customers appreciate value in all its forms.

SOMETIMES WHEN I GET ANGRY, I GET STUPID

Anger makes me want to do things that would feel good in the moment. Then I remember that wearing an orange jumpsuit probably wouldn't flatter me. Anger is normal but most emotion is useless. If you must feel it, channel it. Put a chip on your shoulder and use it before it uses you.

SPEAKING OF STUPID, WHY DOES ANYONE STILL DO THIS?

Speaking of getting stupid and angry, why is anyone still airing their dirty laundry on social media? It never looks good and it never ends well. We've now had almost a decade of data that supports this. Yet people can't seem to help themselves. Twitter and Facebook fights make people look infantile. I guarantee you; with the exception of a few professional athletes and musicians who have yet to mature, no one making seven figures is posting their lunch plans on Facebook or Twitter, let alone arguing.

DO THE HARD THING FIRST

Sometimes knocking down the low hanging fruit first makes sense. But I have found that doing the hard thing first often works best. Otherwise, the hard thing gets left undone. There will always be something easier to do.

DON'T WAIT FOR INSPIRATION

In conjunction with doing the hard thing first, don't wait to be inspired before you act. You won't feel like doing it later either. Great artists practice their art whether they are inspired or not. Great business people read about, think about, and execute business without waiting to be inspired. Not everything you produce is going to come from inspiration or be a home run. Just step up to the plate and swing. Remember, three hits out of 10 at bats will put you into the Hall of Fame... every time.

USE THE POWERFUL QUALITY OF GIVING YOUR ATTENTION

In a world where everyone is competing for attention, giving yours can be a valuable gift. How many times have you had to say something three times and still haven't been heard? How many times have you sent emails that went unread? How many times have you shared something very personal, like a potentially scary medical situation, only to have the person not even remember you told them? The lesson is; you will draw people like a magnet if you actually pay attention to them. Lock in on them and ignore everything else in the environment. People will bond to you and do anything for that quality of attention.

BE A LIGHTHOUSE

A lighthouse doesn't run around seeking boats. It simply radiates light. If you operate this way, what you previously sought will probably find you first.

MAKE THE MOST IMPORTANT THING THE MOST IMPORTANT THING

Focus on what you're doing in the moment. Dismiss the distractions. If you have chosen well, you will be massively productive.

BE AN ANSWER, NOT A QUESTION

Give people value. It's weak to always be showing up to your boss with a question. If you must, at least have a few optional answers they can choose from. If you've ever had anyone following you around asking questions, you know how annoying that can be. You also know how fantastic it can be when someone walks up and hands you an answer to a problem. Be the answer, not the question.

IT'S OKAY TO BE COMPASSIONATE TOWARDS YOURSELF, TOO

You delayed gratification. You practiced self-denial. You didn't overspend or max your credit. You went to college and paid off your loans. You showed up early and stayed late. You didn't blow your money on booze and the lottery. You exhibited the self-discipline and sacrifice necessary to contribute to the tax base and not be a burden to your friends and family. Now some lazy, greedy, self-indulgent, unkempt, would-be poster child for bad decisions, who didn't make the sacrifices you made, thinks that he or she is entitled to your resources. No. Have compassion towards yourself and do not subsidize their bad choices. Too many of you, too often and for too long, have subsidized other people's bad choices. And that's probably the worst choice of all.

CONFIDENCE IS SOMETHING YOU DO, NOT SOMETHING YOU HAVE

While I believe that confidence is born out of achievement, we can approach it a different way as well. Confidence can also be something that you do. Your posture, your breathing and your speech all project confidence. Those are activities. Those are things that you do and you control them. We become what we do – so – "do" confidence!

BEWARE THE AVAILABILITY OF EXCESS

It's not only the failure of the human will that has led us to problems with excess. It's also the availability of food, sex, alcohol, drugs, and communication opportunities. Once we're aware that we can use our will and that we are indeed in the midst of unprecedented opportunities for risk, we can begin to make other choices. We can use our impulse control muscles to take charge – unless we don't want to, in which case, have at it.

EMULATE THE PSYCHOPATH

Psychologist Kevin Dutton has pointed out that many of us could be more successful if we judiciously took on some of the traits of psychopaths. If we were to become more fearless, focused, mindful, mentally tough, charming, action-oriented and occasionally ruthless, we could accomplish much more than we currently do. Think about where those qualities might come in handy – and put them to use. No, I'm not suggesting you become an axe murderer, just a little more productive.

YOUR LIFE IS EITHER AN EXAMPLE – OR A WARNING

You probably watched your parents. Your children and grandchildren are watching you. Do you want your life to be an example? Or would you rather your life serve as an warning?

BE BIGGER THAN WHATEVER HAPPENS TO YOU

Jobs, relationships, possessions, and material wealth can all disappear. Bad stuff can and will happen. Eventually, we will die, so we're going to lose that battle too. I know, very inconvenient. Until then, resolve to push forward through whatever. It's all just grist for the mill. Nil illegitimi carborundum. (Don't let the bastards get you down.) Make your energy superior to misfortune – and even if it's "showing them how to die," resolve to make the last thing you do...the greatest thing you do.

SOME FINAL THOUGHTS

At least in the short term, the future belongs to those who control the public relations and the perception of reality. At some point, perception always becomes reality. For many, it's becoming more difficult to tell the difference between real, virtual, fake and actual competence. I have fallen for this myself. I hired a singer for my band based on her Internet presence before I actually heard her sing in my rehearsal room. Online, she had been "auto-tuned" and sounded great. She had cut CDs and was actually a talented songwriter. In addition, she looked great and could dance like nobody's business. But, the fact is, she was not a particularly terrific singer. I should have been more thorough.

Reality television has made celebrity more important than achievement. In a recent study, when young people were asked what they wanted to be when they grew up, the most prevalent answer was "famous." Professions that require persistent effort that might contribute to society's good were given scant consideration.

It's hard to fault young people for this. They are just looking at the reward system. And on a practical business level, I always advise them to figure out who gets paid and why. I also caution them that companies sometimes promote a list of values but then reward the exact opposite. Of course, the way around that is to simply pay attention and notice what is *actually* valued and rewarded.

Every day we are faced with more stimuli. Researchers note that people are impacted with up to 3,000 marketing messages a day. Everyone is competing for attention. Email keeps coming. The Twitter-sphere is alive with buzz. Instagram grows. Facebook is holding its own. Pinterest lives on. People continue to be distracted from their distraction by distraction.

Those who venture outside walk with their heads down, looking at their phones. In some cases, they are practically living in them. Many use ear buds that allow them to hear music, but keep them from actual, real human contact. The perception is that the world is more connected. In fact, it has become more impersonal and there is evidence that it is becoming more hostile as well.

Growing up in Chicago, we had a name for people who walked the streets with their heads down listening to music. We called them "prey." They were begging to be mugged and in fact, today these folks continually get their phones swiped and wallets stolen. So I urge everyone to wake up, pay attention, be patient and gracious when possible, and be part of a greater solution, not part of a greater problem.

Why do I bring up these issues? I mention these because if you're over sixty, society still needs you – perhaps now more than ever. In a world that values celebrity over achievement, your competence, experience, wisdom and toughness give you a competitive advantage. In addition, how will young people learn about service and sacrifice if they never see it? It may be time for all of us to be strong for someone else. What kind of service can we still provide? What kind of positive difference can we make?

You may argue that you've been doing that all of your life. If you have, I applaud you. And you of all people then know of the times when you had the greatest strength. You of all people know that the more we think about ourselves, the weaker we become. The more we are concerned with others, the greater load we seem to be able to carry. When I am consumed with my own situation, I succumb to self-pity, anger and fear. When I am consumed with a mission larger than myself, I get stronger.

I'm not talking about rescuing or saving the world. I'm talking about deliberate, targeted service. That might mean helping one young person pay for college, mentoring someone, or volunteering at a hospital.

We can all find ways to serve. We can mentor, coach, teach, volunteer, funnel money to a charity and find a hundred other ways to be useful. We begin by sweeping our own front porch and then working out towards the street.

I encourage everyone to remember where they came from. Let's not forget our history and what we've overcome to get where we are. If you're still standing and still motivated, you've overcome. But don't settle. Get into it. Dig in. Be badass! Show up!

The world still needs you. Grab your swag and embrace the challenge of your choosing.

If you do that, perhaps you can make the last thing you ever do your greatest gift – and maybe even your greatest adventure.

APPENDIX

My Personal Over-60 Hall of Fame

The people listed below are all over 60 years of age and still crushing it. If you wish to know more about any of these folks, each has an extensive Internet presence. They are all people I admire.

Stanley McChrystal – Retired Four-star General, former Commander of JSOC and ISAF

James Webb – Marine Veteran, Author, Screenwriter, former U.S. Senator and Secretary of the Navy

Lee Child – Author

Chuck Norris – Actor and Martial Artist

Bruce Springsteen – Musician

Liam Neeson – Actor

Denzel Washington – Actor

Buddy Guy – Musician

B.B. King - Musician

Sylvester Stallone – Actor

Tony Bennett – Musician and Painter

Dr. Khosro Khalogli – Real Estate Tycoon and Fitness Expert

Dr. Floyd Hoelting –University of Texas, Executive Director of Housing and Food Services

Jonathan Goldsmith – Actor (The Most Interesting Man in the World)

Danny Trejo – Actor

Pete Carroll – Seattle Seahawk Head Football Coach

Bob Kerrey – Former Navy SEAL, former Governor and former U.S. Senator

Tony Danza – Actor

Gene Simmons – Businessman and Musician

Sting – Musician

Jon Kabat-Zinn – Author and Mindfulness Meditation Expert

Mark Sisson – Fitness Expert and Proponent of the Paleo Diet

Steve Maxwell – Fitness Authority and Martial Arts Instructor

Brian Auger – Musician

Robert Lamm – Musician

List of Outstanding Reference Books

I want to extend thanks to some of the amazing people who have shared many valuable lessons with me. Not coincidentally, most have performed extraordinary military service. For each, I've listed at least one of the books they've authored that I have benefitted from. They are:

<u>My Share of the Task</u> by Stan McChrystal (Retired Four-star General; Former Leader of JSOC and ISAF)

<u>Unleash the Warrior Within</u> by Richard "Mack" Machowicz (Former U.S. Navy SEAL)

<u>No-Excuse Leadership</u> by Brace Barber (Former U.S. Army Ranger)

<u>I Heard My Country Calling</u> by James Webb (Former Marine, former Secretary of the Navy, former U.S. Senator)

<u>The Heart and the Fist</u> by Eric Greitans (Former U.S. Navy SEAL)

<u>The Intuitive Warrior</u> by Michael Jaco (Former U.S. Navy SEAL)

<u>The Way of the SEAL</u> by Mark Divine (Former U.S. Navy SEAL)

Take Control by Michael Janke (Former U.S. Navy SEAL)

Relentless: From Good to Great to Unstoppable by Tim Grover

If you would like Lee Witt to speak to your company or organization, please contact Terry Quick (425-670-0888) at Entco International, Inc. for details.

More information on Lee Witt can be found at:

www.brickhouseleadership.com

www.brickhouseband.com